Unnatural Disasters

JANET N. ABRAMOVITZ

Linda Starke, *Editor*

WORLDWATCH PAPER 158

October 2001

THE WORLDWATCH INSTITUTE is an independent, nonprofit environmental research organization in Washington, DC. Its mission is to foster a sustainable society in which human needs are met in ways that do not threaten the health of the natural environment or future generations. To this end, the Institute conducts interdisciplinary research on emerging global issues, the results of which are published and disseminated to decision-makers and the media.

FINANCIAL SUPPORT for the Institute is provided by the Geraldine R. Dodge Foundation, the Ford Foundation, the Richard & Rhoda Goldman Fund, the William and Flora Hewlett Foundation, W. Alton Jones Foundation, Charles Stewart Mott Foundation, the Curtis and Edith Munson Foundation, David and Lucile Packard Foundation, John D. and Catherine T. MacArthur Foundation, Summit Foundation, Surdna Foundation, Inc., Turner Foundation, Inc., U.N. Environment Programme, U.N. Population Fund, Wallace Genetic Foundation, Wallace Global Fund, Weeden Foundation, and the Winslow Foundation. The Institute also receives financial support from its Council of Sponsors members—Tom and Cathy Crain, James and Deanna Dehlsen, Roger and Vicki Sant, Robert Wallace and Raisa Scriabine, and Eckart Wintzen—and from the many other friends of Worldwatch.

THE WORLDWATCH PAPERS provide in-depth, quantitative and qualitative analysis of the major issues affecting prospects for a sustainable society. The Papers are written by members of the Worldwatch Institute research staff and reviewed by experts in the field. Regularly published in five languages, they have been used as concise and authoritative references by governments, nongovernmental organizations, and educational institutions worldwide. For a partial list of available Papers, see back pages.

Table of Contents

ACKNOWLEDGMENTS: My most sincere thanks to the following reviewers for their thoughtful comments on drafts of this Paper: Susan Cutter, Robert Hamilton, Ailsa Holloway, Mary Fran Myers, Roger Pielke, Jr., Jonathan Walter, and the eminent Gilbert White. Thanks also to the following individuals and organizations for providing data: Angelika Wertz of Munich Re, Caroline Michellier and CRED, and Susan Pfiffner of the International Federation of Red Cross and Red Crescent Societes.

Thanks to colleagues at Worldwatch: Liz Doherty for artful layout and design; Denise Warden for coordinating production; Chris Flavin, Seth Dunn, and Gary Gardner, and others for review; Danielle Nierenberg for proofreading; and Dick Bell, Leanne Mitchell, and Niki Clark for communications and outreach. Many thanks to Linda Starke for her expert editing. Special thanks to Michael Montag, whose outstanding research assistance, data wrestling, and proofreading helped me through the lion's share of the project, and to Kathleen Huvane for help at the end. This Paper is dedicated to the memory of my parents.

JANET N. ABRAMOVITZ is a Senior Researcher at the Worldwatch Institute, where her research focuses on ecosystem services, forests and forest products, biodiversity, freshwater ecosystems, consumption, and social equity. She is a co-author of the Institute's yearly *State of the World* and *Vital Signs,* and of the joint Worldwatch/World Resources atlas *Watersheds of the World.*

Prior to joining Worldwatch in 1995, she had over a decade of experience working at World Resources Institute, the International Institute for Environment and Development, and other governmental and non-governmental organizations. Ms. Abramovitz earned a Master of Science degree from the University of Maryland Department of Botany in ecology and statistics in 1983.

Introduction

In December 1999, 15 million cubic meters of mud, trees, and boulders came barreling down from Venezuela's coastal mountain range onto the densely populated and heavily urbanized ribbon of land that hugs the Caribbean coast, killing some 30,000 people and causing about $2 billion in damages. Two years worth of rain had fallen in just two days, dislodging soil already saturated by two weeks of heavy La Niña rains. While floods and landslides are common in this area, the devastation unearthed far more than boulders and bare soil. It exposed the perils of development in risky locations and inadequate disaster planning and response—dangerous debris that are far more difficult to clear away.[1]

One year earlier, Hurricane Mitch slammed into Central America, pummeling Honduras, Nicaragua, El Salvador, and Guatemala for more than a week in October. As the powerful storm hung over the region, it dumped as much as two meters (80 inches) of rain. By the time it turned back out to sea, some 10,000 people had died, making Mitch the deadliest hurricane in 200 years. Conservative estimates place its damage to the region at around $8.5 billion—higher than the combined gross domestic product (GDP) of Honduras and Nicaragua, the two nations hardest hit. The storm set back development in the region by decades.[2]

But Venezuela and Central America were not the only regions to experience such devastation in recent years. In fact, the 1990s set a new record for disasters worldwide.

During the decade over $608 billion in economic losses was chalked up to natural catastrophes, an amount greater than during the previous four decades combined.[3]

In 1998–99 alone, over 120,000 people were killed and millions were displaced from their homes. In India, 10,000 people lost their lives in a 1998 cyclone in Gujarat; the following year as many as 50,000 died when a "supercyclone" hit Orissa. Vast forest fires raged out of control in Brazil, Indonesia, and Siberia. The deadly landslides in Venezuela in December 1999 capped off the disastrous decade.[4]

The new millennium began with back-to-back earthquakes in El Salvador in January 2001, which erased much of the reconstruction efforts made there in the two-and-a-half years since Hurricane Mitch. That same month, powerful earthquakes struck Gujarat. And major floods submerged much of Mozambique for the second year in a row.[5]

Ironically, the United Nations had designated the 1990s as the International Decade for Natural Disaster Reduction, hoping to stem the rising toll taken by natural disasters. Instead, the 1990s may go down in history as the International Decade *of* Disasters, as the world experienced the most costly spate of floods, storms, earthquakes, and fires ever.

Around the world, a growing share of the devastation triggered by "natural" disasters stems from ecologically destructive practices and from putting ourselves in harm's way. Many ecosystems have been frayed to the point where they are no longer resilient and able to withstand natural disturbances, setting the stage for "unnatural disasters"—those made more frequent or more severe due to human actions. By degrading forests, engineering rivers, filling in wetlands, and destabilizing the climate, we are unraveling the strands of a complex ecological safety net. We are beginning to understand just how valuable that safety net is.

The enormous expansion of the human population and our built environment in the twentieth century means that more people and more economic activities are vulnerable. The migration of people to cities and coasts also increases our vulnerability to the full array of natural hazards. The explosive growth of shantytowns in the cities of the developing world puts untold numbers of people at risk. And these human-exacerbated disasters often take their heaviest toll on those who can least afford it—the poor.

Ecologically, socially, and economically, many regions are now vulnerable and ill prepared for the onslaught of storms, floods, and other hazards. Hurricane Mitch washed away hillsides, sweeping up homes, farms, roads, bridges, and people in massive mudslides and floods. Given that Central America has frequent hurricanes and earthquakes as well as some of the highest rates of deforestation in the world—each year it loses 2–4 percent of its remaining forest cover, and Honduras alone has already cleared half its forested land—the tragedy should not really be all that surprising. The pressures of poverty, population growth, and inequitable land rights had forced more and more people into vulnerable areas such as steep hillsides and unprotected riverbanks. The lion's share of farmland is owned by a tiny fraction of the population. In Guatemala, for example, 65 percent of the farmland is held by less than 3 percent of the farms. In Honduras, 90 percent of prime farmland is owned by 10 percent of the population. Little wonder that 82 percent of the rural population in Honduras and over two thirds in Guatemala and Nicaragua now live on the fragile hillsides. Further, when crippling debt burdens consume most of a nation's budget and stall development, few resources remain to address these problems.[6]

To date, much of the response to disasters has focused on improving weather predictions before the events and providing cleanup and humanitarian relief afterward, both of which have without doubt helped save many lives. Yet much more can be done. On average, $1 invested in mitigation can save $7 in disaster recovery costs. And mitigation measures are far more effective when integrated into sustainable development efforts. Nature provides many valuable services for free; healthy and resilient ecosystems are shock absorbers that protect against coastal storms and sponges that soak up floodwaters, for instance. We should take advantage of these free services rather than undermine them. In order to stem the ever rising social and economic costs of disasters, we need to focus on how to mitigate disasters by understanding our own culpability, taking steps to reduce our vulnerability, and managing our impacts on nature more wisely.[7]

Counting Disasters

During the twentieth century, more than 10 million people died from natural catastrophes, according to Munich Re, a reinsurer that undertakes global data collection and analysis of these trends. Its natural catastrophe data include floods, storms, earthquakes, fires, and the like. Excluded are industrial or technological disasters (such as oil spills and nuclear accidents), insect infestations, epidemics, and most droughts.[8]

While some 500–850 natural disaster events are recorded every year, only a few are classified by Munich Re as "great"—natural catastrophes that result in deaths or losses so high as to require outside assistance. Over the past 50 years there has been a dramatic increase in this type of disaster. In the 1950s there were 20 "great" catastrophes, in the 1970s there were 47, and by the 1990s there were 86. (See Figure 1.)[9]

The total number of disasters (not just "great" ones) has also been on the rise, with the year 2000 setting a new record—850 disasters, according to Munich Re, topping 1999's record of 750. The average for the 1990s was 650 disasters per year.[10]

Between 1985 and 1999, nearly 561,000 people died in natural disasters, according to data collected by Munich Re. Only 4 percent of the fatalities were in industrial countries. The company reported that 77 percent of the deaths were in Asia, 10 percent in South America, 4 percent each in Africa and Central America, 2 percent in the Caribbean, and over

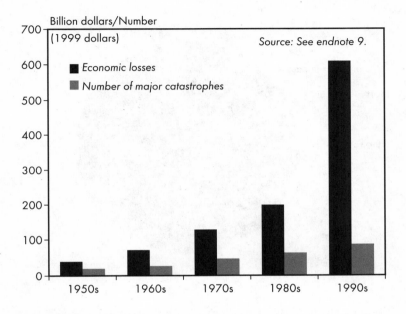

FIGURE 1

Rising Tide of Major Disasters, by Decade

Billion dollars/Number

(1999 dollars)   Source: See endnote 9.

■ Economic losses
■ Number of major catastrophes

1950s   1960s   1970s   1980s   1990s

1 percent each in Europe and North America. (See Figure 2.) Worldwide, half of all deaths were due to floods. (See Figure 3.) Earthquakes were the second biggest killer, claiming 169,000 lives. Between 1985 and 1999, 37 percent of the recorded events were windstorms, 28 percent floods, and 15 percent earthquakes. Events such as fires and landslides accounted for the remaining 20 percent.[11]

Asia has been especially hard hit. The region is large and heavily populated, particularly in dangerous coastal areas. There is frequent seismic, tropical storm, and flood activity. Asia's natural and social vulnerability is borne out by the statistics. Between 1985 and 1999, Asia suffered 77 percent of all deaths, 90 percent of all those affected by disasters, and 45 percent of all recorded economic losses due to disasters.[12]

As tragic as the death toll of recent years is, in earlier decades and centuries it was not uncommon to lose hun-

FIGURE 2

Global Deaths from Disasters, by Region, 1985–99

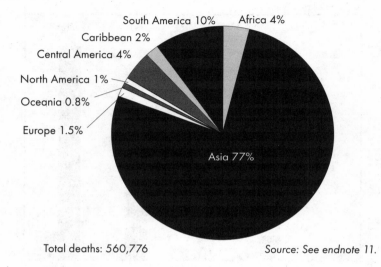

Total deaths: 560,776   Source: See endnote 11.

dreds of thousands of lives in a single great catastrophe. In the last 20 years, however, there has been only one such event—the cyclone and storm surge that hit Bangladesh in 1991 and took 139,000 lives.[13]

Early warnings and disaster preparedness have been a significant factor in keeping the death toll of recent decades from reaching even higher. So, too, have advances in basic services, such as clean water and sanitation. Following disasters, the life-saving benefits are apparent. According to the Chinese government, 90 percent of the 30,000 deaths from floods in 1954 were a result of communicable diseases like dysentery, typhoid, and cholera that struck in the following weeks and months. After the 1998 Yangtze flood, in contrast, no such epidemics were reported (although diarrheal diseases were common). Nevertheless, increased incidence of diseases like diarrhea, malaria, cholera, and dengue following disasters remains a problem. The World

FIGURE 3

Global Deaths by Disaster Type, 1985–99

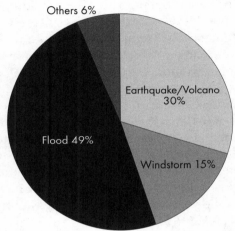

Others 6%

Earthquake/Volcano 30%

Flood 49%

Windstorm 15%

Total deaths: 560,776   Source: See endnote 11.

Health Organization reports that in Africa, for example, people displaced by disasters or conflict are far more likely to contract malaria.[14]

While the death toll per event has declined in recent decades, the number of people affected has grown. In the last decade over 2 billion people worldwide have been affected by disasters, about 211 million people per year (some of these may be affected and counted more than once). Ninety percent of the affected people were in Asia and 6 percent in Africa. More people are now displaced by disasters than by conflict, according to the *World Disasters Report*.[15]

Worldwide, floods cause nearly one third of all economic losses and 70 percent of all homelessness, as well as half of all deaths, according to Munich Re. Damaging floods have become more frequent and more severe. They are the type of disaster that people have the greatest hand in exacerbating. In China's Hunan province, for instance, historical records show that whereas in early centuries flooding occurred once every 20 years or so, it now occurs 9 out of every 10 years. In Europe, flooding on the Rhine River has worsened as a result of changes in the way the river is managed. At the German border town of Karlsruhe, prior to 1977 the Rhine rose 7.62 meters above flood level only four times since 1900. Between 1977 and 1995 it reached that level 10 times. In the United States, major flooding on the Mississippi River and its tributaries has also grown more frequent and severe, as will be discussed later.[16]

Although there has been some success in reducing the death toll, the financial toll of disasters has reached catastrophic proportions. Measured in 1999 dollars, the $608 billion in economic losses during the 1990s was more than three times the figure in the 1980s, almost nine times that in the 1960s, and more than 15 times the total in the 1950s. The biggest single year for losses in history was 1995, when damages reached $157 billion. An earthquake in Kobe, Japan, accounted for more than two thirds of that total. For weather-related disasters, 1998 was the biggest year on record, at nearly $93 billion in recorded losses, with China's Yangtze River flood absorbing more than a third of this total. Munich Re's Dr. Gerhard Berz has noted that because damage figures only include the major disasters, the total losses would likely be at least twice as high if the hundreds of lesser events that occur each year were included.[17]

The economic losses measured usually include insured property losses, the costs of repairing physical infrastructure like roads and power, and some crop losses. Such direct losses are the easiest to measure. But the tally rarely includes indirect or secondary impacts, such as the costs of business failures or interruptions, suicide due to despair, domestic violence, human health effects, or lost human and development potential. Losses in developing countries are particularly undercounted. Damage figures also exclude the destruction of natural resources. Failure to measure secondary impact and natural resources is common in economic assessments in the best of times; after disasters, it is even more difficult.[18]

Between 1985 and 1999, Asia sustained 45 percent of the world's economic losses to disasters, North America 33 percent, and Europe 12 percent. (See Figure 4.) Rural areas and developing nations are in general underrepresented in global disaster data, as reporting systems tend to be weaker. Africa is particularly underrepresented because it is rarely hit by major storms or earthquakes. Most of the disasters in Africa are slow-onset disasters, like droughts, or smaller events that are not counted in the global tallies. The region also has less infrastructure and capital exposure, so it escapes the notice of the global insurance industry.[19]

Economic losses can be especially devastating to poor countries. As in Honduras and Nicaragua after Hurricane Mitch, disaster losses often represent a large share of the national economy. While the wealthiest countries sustained 57.3 percent of the measured economic losses to disasters between 1985 and 1999, this represented only 2.5 percent of

FIGURE 4

Global Economic Losses from Disasters, by Region, 1985–99

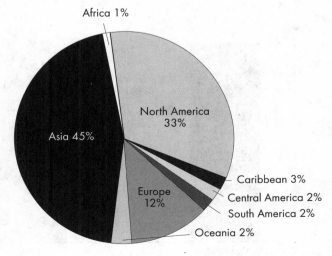

Total Economic Losses: $918.7 billion   *Source: See endnote 19.*

their GDP. (See Figure 5.) In contrast, the poorest countries endured 24.4 percent of the economic toll of disasters, which added up to a whopping 13.4 percent of their GDP, further increasing their vulnerability to future disasters. And in the poorest countries, little if any of the losses are insured. Worldwide, only one fifth of all disaster losses were insured. The vast majority of insured losses, some 92 percent, were in industrial nations. Finding a way to provide a financial safety net for developing countries is of critical importance.[20]

The quickly rising economic toll, the troubling increase in the number of major catastrophes that overwhelm nations, and the prospect of more extreme weather events due to climate change provide clear evidence that a new way of managing nature and ourselves is in order.

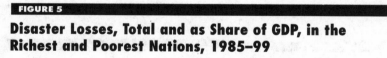

Disaster Losses, Total and as Share of GDP, in the Richest and Poorest Nations, 1985–99

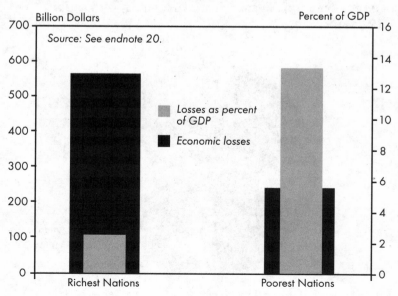

Ecological Vulnerability

There is an important distinction between natural and unnatural disasters. Many ecosystems and species are adapted to natural disturbance, and indeed disturbances are necessary to maintain their health and vitality, and even their continued existence. Many forests and grasslands, for instance, are adapted to periodic natural fires, and need them to burn off dead vegetation, restore soil fertility, and release seeds.

Likewise, river systems need periodic flooding, and plants and animals across the landscape are adapted to this regime. Fish use the floodplain as a spawning ground and nursery for their young. Some fish consume and disburse seeds, which can sustain them for an entire year. Many plants need the flood period to germinate and absorb newly available dissolved nutrients. Migratory birds also rely on the bounty that floods bring. Soils, too, benefit from the regular addition of nutrients and organic matter, and underground aquifers are refilled as floodwaters are slowly absorbed into the ground. But by disrupting the natural flooding regime, we cut off the interactions between a river and its surrounding landscape—interactions that make them more diverse and productive. Indeed, natural flooding is so beneficial that some of the biggest fish and crop harvests come the year after a flood. Little wonder that floodplains and deltas have attracted human settlement for millennia and been the cradles of civilizations.[21]

Just as not every natural disturbance is a disaster, not every disaster is completely natural. We have altered so many natural systems so dramatically that their ability to bounce back from disturbance has been greatly diminished. Deforestation impairs watersheds, raises the risk of fires, and contributes to climate change. Destruction of coastal wetlands, dunes, and mangroves eliminates nature's shock absorbers for coastal storms. Such human-made changes end up making naturally vulnerable areas—such as hillsides, rivers, coastal zones, and low-lying islands—even more vulnerable to extreme weather events.

Droughts, and the famines that often follow, may be the most widely understood—if underreported—example of an unnatural disaster. They are triggered partly by global climate variability (both natural and human-induced) and partly by resource mismanagement such as deforestation, overgrazing, and the overtapping of rivers and wells for irrigation. Considered slow-onset events, droughts are not as well reported as rapid-onset events like storms and floods, nor are they usually included in disaster-related financial loss data. Yet they affect major portions of Africa and Asia and are projected to continue worsening in the coming years as a result of climate change. According to data prepared by the Centre for Research on the Epidemiology of Disasters and published in the *World Disasters Report*, droughts and famines accounted for 42 percent of disaster-related deaths between 1991 and 2000. (Munich Re does not include most droughts in its count of disaster-related deaths, so its data cannot be compared to these figures.)[22]

Human settlements, too, have become less resilient as we put more structures, more economic activity, and more people in vulnerable places. Our usual approach to natural disturbances is to try to prevent them through shortsighted strategies using methods that all too often exacerbate them. Dams and levees, for example, change the flow of rivers and can increase the frequency and severity of floods and droughts.

China's Yangtze River dramatically shows the consequences of the loss of healthy ecosystems. The flooding in 1998 caused more than 4,000 deaths, affected 223 million people, inundated 25 million hectares of cropland, and cost well over $36 billion. Heavy summer rains are common in southern and central China, and flooding often ensues. But in 1998, as the floodwater continued to rise, it became clear that other factors besides heavy rains were at play. One influence was the extensive deforestation that had left many steep hillsides bare. Indeed, in the past few decades 85 percent of the forest cover in the Yangtze basin has been cleared by logging and agriculture. The loss of forests, which normally intercept rainfall and allow it to be absorbed by the soil, permitted water to rush across the land, carrying valuable topsoil with it. As the runoff raced across the denuded landscape, it caused floods.[23]

In addition, the Yangtze's natural flood controls had been undermined by numerous dams and levees, and a large proportion of the basin's wetlands and lakes, which usually act as natural "sponges," had been filled in or drained. The areas previously left open to give floodwaters a place to go have filled instead with waves of human settlements. All these changes reduced the capacity of the Yangtze's watershed to absorb rain, and greatly increased the speed and severity of the resulting runoff.[24]

In the U.S. Pacific Northwest, 94 percent of landslides originated from clearcuts and logging roads.

Chinese government officials initially denied that the Yangtze floods were anything but natural, claiming that the flooding was caused by El Niño. But as the disaster toll mounted, the State Council finally recognized the human element. It banned logging in the upper Yangtze watershed, prohibited additional land reclamation projects in the river's floodplain, and stepped up efforts to reforest the watershed.[25]

Flooding and landslides following deforestation are not limited to developing countries. In the U.S. Pacific Northwest, where hundreds of landslides now occur annually, a study found that 94 percent of them originated from clearcuts and logging roads. The torrents of water and debris from degraded watersheds caused billions of dollars in damage in 1996 alone.[26]

Paradoxically, clearing natural forests also exacerbates drought in dry years by allowing the soil to dry out more quickly. Such droughts helped fuel the record-breaking fires in Indonesia and Brazil in 1997–98. These massive fires occurred in tropical forests that are normally too moist to burn. But when fragmented by logging and agricultural clearing, the forests dried to the point where fires set deliberately to clear land were quickly able to spread out of control. In Indonesia, industrial timber and palm oil plantation owners took advantage of a severe El Niño drought to expand their areas and in 1997–98 burned at least 9.8 million hectares, an area the size of South Korea.[27]

The smoke and haze from Indonesia's fires choked neighboring countries, affecting about 70 million people. The economic damage to the region has been conservatively estimated at about $9.3 billion. Schools, airports, and businesses were shut down. Many crops were lost to the drought and fires, and the haze impaired the pollination of other crops and wild plants, the ecological repercussions of which will unfold for many years. If harm to fisheries, biodiversity, orangutans, and long-term health were included, the damage figure would be far higher.[28]

Sumatra and Kalimantan, the provinces where most of the 1997–98 fires occurred, have lost up to 30 percent of their forest cover to exploitation and fire in just the last 15 years. One of the first smoke signals that indicated that the forests were in trouble due to exploitation policies was seen during another El Niño year, 1982–83, when 3.2 million hectares burned in Kalimantan. In 1991, another half-million hectares burned, and in 1994 almost 4.9 million hectares went up in smoke. As Charles Barber and James Schweithelm put it in *Trial by Fire*, a study of Indonesia, "the fires of 1997 and 1998 were just the latest symptom of a destructive forest resource management system carried out by the Suharto regime over 30 years."[29]

In South Africa, the spread of non-native vegetation (including pine and wattle trees) has greatly increased the incidence of intense and dangerous fires. The invasives are also hijacking precious water resources—some 7 percent of the annual surface water flow—and displacing globally unique native plant communities. Alien plants already cover some 10 million hectares—about 8 percent of the vast nation. A serious effort is under way in South Africa to stop the spread of invasive species, which, unless checked, are predicted to double in area in the next 20 years.[30]

In contrast to the human-made unnatural disasters that should be prevented but are not, considerable effort is spent trying to stop natural disturbances that are actually beneficial. The result is disasters of unnatural proportions. In the United States, for example, fire suppression has long been the policy, even in forest and grassland ecosystems that are fire-dependent. The result has been the buildup of debris that fuels very hot fires capable of destroying these ecosystems—and the homes that are increasingly built there. The record-setting cost of fires and fire-suppression in the United States—nearly $1.4 billion in federal agency costs alone in 2000—is a telling reminder of the consequences of such wrongheaded policies. Recent events have rekindled the debate, and are providing the stimulus to rethink U.S. fire policies.[31]

Likewise, a common response to floods is to try to prevent them by controlling rivers. But contrary to popular belief, containing a river in embankments, dams, channels, reservoirs, and other structures does not reduce flooding. Instead, it dramatically increases the rate of flow, and causes even worse flooding downstream. The Rhine River, for example, is cut off from 90 percent of its original floodplain in its upper reaches, and flows twice as fast as it did before the modifications. Flooding in the basin has grown significantly more frequent and severe due to increased urbanization, river engineering, and poor floodplain management.[32]

The Great Midwest Flood of the upper Mississippi and Missouri rivers in 1993 provided another dramatic and costly lesson on the effects of treating the natural flow of rivers as a pathological condition. The flood was the largest and most destructive in modern U.S. history. It set records for amounts of precipitation, upland runoff, river levels, flood duration, area of flooding, and economic loss. Financial costs were estimated at $19 billion. The floodwaters breached levees spanning nearly 10,000 kilometers. In hindsight, many now realize that the river was simply attempting to reclaim its floodplain. Not surprisingly, 1993 was a record spawning year for fish as the river was restored, temporarily, to more natural functioning.[33]

Today's problems reflect the cumulative impacts of more than a century of actions by public and private interests to expand agriculture, facilitate navigation, and control flooding on the Mississippi and its tributaries. Nearly half of the 3,782-kilometer-long Mississippi flows through artificial channels. Records show that the 1973, 1982, and 1993 floods were substantially higher than they might have been before structural flood control began in 1927 after a major flood.[34]

Throughout the huge Mississippi River basin, the construction of thousands of levees, the creation of deep navigation channels, extensive farming in the floodplain, and the draining of more than 6.9 million hectares of wetlands (more than an 85-percent reduction in some states) have cut into the ability of the Mississippi's floodplains to absorb and slowly release rain, floodwater, nutrients, and sediments. Separating fish from their floodplain spawning grounds and upstream reaches has virtually eliminated some species and caused many others to decline. The commercial fish catch in the Missouri River, the Mississippi's largest tributary, fell 83 percent between 1947 and 1995.[35]

Flood control and navigation structures have also adversely affected the Mississippi Delta and the Gulf of Mexico. Because these structures trap sediments rather than allow them to be carried downstream to replenish the delta, as they have done for millennia, the coastal areas are actually subsiding as water inundates wetlands and threatens coastal communities and productive fisheries.[36]

The management and policy changes begun after the 1927 flood have had other perverse effects. One was to shift the cost and responsibility for flood control and relief from the local to the federal level. Another was to encourage people, farms, and businesses to settle in vulnerable areas with the knowledge that they would be bailed out of trouble at taxpayer expense.[37]

The government also fostered settlement in vulnerable areas by providing crop insurance and crop price guarantees, and by paying for most of the cost of levees. The net result is that farming the land in the former river channel is profitable only with regular federal payments for flood damage.[38]

In 1968, Congress created the National Flood Insurance Program (NFIP) to cover flood-prone areas that private insurers deemed too risky. Unfortunately, this led to rebuilding in many of these areas. Nearly half of the payments for flood claims went to the repeat flood victims who account for less than 1 percent of the policyholders. And for those without flood insurance, emergency relief aid was repeatedly provided, further contributing to the cycle of losses.[39]

The 1993 Mississippi flood's human and economic costs, combined with its benefits to the ecosystem's functions, inspired a rethinking of the way large rivers are managed. After the flood, a federal task force recommended ending the nation's over-reliance on engineering and structural means for flood control in favor of floodplain restoration and management. It emphasized managing the river as a whole ecosystem rather than as short segments. Other reforms to the NFIP have been promoted by a wide range of groups (from floodplain managers to insurance companies and environmental groups) to reduce repeated flood losses, save taxpayer dollars, and restore the health of the Mississippi basin.[40]

The 1993 Mississippi flood's costs inspired a rethinking of the way large rivers are managed.

On the other side of the globe, Bangladesh suffered its most extensive flood of the century in the summer of 1998, when two thirds of the country was inundated for months. Annual floods are a natural and beneficial cycle in this low-lying coastal nation, which encircles the meandering deltas of the Ganges, Brahmaputra, and Meghna Rivers. The people of Bangladesh have long adapted their housing, land use patterns, and economic activities to these "barsha" or beneficial floods. However, 1998 brought a "bonna" or devastating flood. Floodwaters reached near-record levels and did not recede for months. All told, 1,300 people died, 31 million people were left temporarily homeless, and 16,000 kilometers of roads were heavily damaged. Overall damage estimates exceed $3.4 billion—or 10 percent of the nation's GDP.[41]

A number of factors precipitated Bangladesh's bonna flood. Heavy rainfall upriver in the Himalayas of north India and Nepal, some of which fell on heavily logged areas, exacerbated the disaster, as did the runoff from extensive development upstream that helped clog the region's rivers and floodplains with silt and mud. In the future, climate change will make Bangladesh even more vulnerable, as rising sea levels are projected to submerge 20 percent of the nation's land area and increased extreme rainfall and cyclone activity could bring more flooding. This problem will be made worse because large expanses of stabilizing mangroves have been removed from shores in recent years to make way for shrimp ponds, exposing the coast to more inundation.[42]

Further, a major reason that so much of Bangladesh was submerged for so long was that extensive embankments built in the last 10 years as part of the nation's Flood Action Plan actually prevented the drainage of water, because water that topped the embankment during the flood's peak could not drain as the river water receded. (The structures also dried out the backwaters that once fertilized fields and provided fish after the floods receded.) While the Bangladeshi peasants look at most floods as beneficial, engineers and donors tend to see all flooding as a problem to be solved by technical measures. As researcher Thomas Hofer has noted, "when it comes to perception of floods and their danger, few heed the wisdom of villagers, even though it is they who have to (mostly) live with the flood."[43]

Social Vulnerability

Some places and some people are more vulnerable to natural hazards. Growing concentrations of people and infrastructure in vulnerable areas like coasts, floodplains, and unstable slopes mean that more people and economic activities are in harm's way. While poor countries are more vulnerable, in every nation some people and communities—notably the very poor, women, and ethnic minorities—are especially hard hit during and after disasters. For poorer countries and poorer people, disasters can take a disproportionately large share of income and resources. Misplaced development priorities and heavy debt burdens can exacerbate disasters and cripple recovery efforts, further hampering development.

Two major global social trends of recent decades have increased our vulnerability to natural hazards: the migration of people to coasts and cities, and the enormous expansion of the built environment. Approximately 37 percent of the world's population—more than 2 billion people—lives within 100 kilometers of a coastline. Coastal zones are especially vulnerable to storms, high winds, flooding, erosion, tidal waves, and the effects of inland flooding. In the U.S. Atlantic and Gulf coasts, the areas most exposed to hurricanes, 47 percent of the population lives in coastal counties. Between 1950 and 1991, a period of relatively few hurricanes, the population of South Florida exploded from under 3 million people to more than 13 million. And 80 percent of this growth occurred in coastal regions. When Hurricane Andrew hit in 1992, it therefore struck a densely populated region.[44]

Similarly, there has been explosive growth of cities. Since 1950, the world's urban population has increased nearly fourfold. Today, the urban population—almost half the people in the world—is growing three times faster than the rural population. Many cities are also in coastal areas, further compounding the risks. Of the world's 19 megacities—those with over 10 million inhabitants—13 are in coastal zones.[45]

As the built environment increases in amount and density, potential losses increase. As the *World Disasters Report* puts it, "growing cities concentrate risk." Urban areas are dense concentrations not only of people but also buildings, roads, rail lines, pipelines, communications systems, and water and sanitary services. The concentration of these "lifelines" means that a disruption in service can affect a very large share of a region's population and economic activity. The earthquake that rocked Kobe, Japan, in 1995 killed 6,350 people and cost over $100 billion, making it the most expensive natural disaster in history. It disrupted the region's economic activity for months, including vital shipping and railway lines.[46]

Urbanization also increases the risk of flooding. When land is covered by impervious surfaces such as roads and roofs, the frequency and severity of flash floods increase. Urbanizing 50 percent of a watershed can increase the frequency of floods from once every 100 years to once every 5 years.[47]

In much of the developing world, urbanization has additional dangers. A good deal of the growth is unplanned, unregulated, and unregistered. In Venezuela, for instance, the little urban or land use planning that exists is disregarded. Up to half the people in the largest cities of the developing world live in unplanned squatter colonies, which are often sited in vulnerable areas such as floodplains and hillsides or even garbage dumps. These poorer communities are far less likely to have public services such as water, sanitation, storm drains, and health and emergency services. As a result, when disasters strike, the residents are even worse off. After disasters they have few, if any, resources to fall back on to survive and rebuild.[48]

Whether in urban or rural areas, the poorest and most marginalized suffer the most. A disproportionate number of the world's poor live on the front line of exposure to disasters. In Venezuela, 54 percent were below the poverty line before the landslides hit. In Nicaragua, 80 percent of those who lost their homes during Hurricane Mitch were living at or below the poverty line even before the storm, and as noted earlier, the vast majority of the rural population in the Mitch-savaged nations lives on and farms fragile mountainous slopes. [49]

In Central America, the nations most ravaged by Mitch—Guatemala, Honduras, and Nicaragua—have a history of highly inequitable distribution of land and wealth. Such extreme poverty invites disaster. In the Honduran capital of Tegucigalpa, one neighborhood that slid into the Choluteca River was home to vendors from the local market who had cobbled together shanties for lack of affordable housing. In the countryside, where prime agricultural land was being used mostly to produce export commodities such as bananas and coffee, the small farmers who produce beans and corn—the staples of domestic consumption—had been forced onto steep hillsides, where they were much more vulnerable to massive erosion and landslides.[50]

Central American farmers who used sustainable farming methods fared far better during the hurricane than conventional farmers.

Interestingly, Central American farmers who used agroecological (sustainable) farming methods fared far better during the hurricane than conventional farmers. According to a post-disaster survey of nearly 2,000 farms in the regions, farmers who used sustainable practices (which emphasize soil and water conservation) experienced very little erosion and retained far more precious topsoil than conventional farms. When an entire hillside or watershed uses agroecological practices, the movement of soils and water that causes landslides at lower elevations can be prevented.[51]

After the storm, half the people in Honduras had lost their homes or been evacuated and 70 percent were without clean water. More than 70 percent of the crops were destroyed—in a nation where two thirds of the workers are in agriculture, which accounts for half of export revenue.

Nicaragua suffered similarly large losses. Nutrient-rich top-soil was also lost, and it will be years before many fields can be rehabilitated and crops can bear fruit. Thousands of land mines, planted during a decade of civil conflict, were washed to unknown locations.[52]

The United Nations estimated that Mitch set the region's development back by 20 years. The cost of rebuilding infrastructure in Honduras and Nicaragua alone was estimated at nearly $9 billion. But far from starting with a clean economic slate, Central American nations face the impossible task of rebuilding while paying the development debt of previous decades. Already over $10 billion in debt before the disaster, Honduras and Nicaragua were together paying $2.2 million a day simply to service their existing debts.[53]

After Mitch, the World Bank quickly arranged a large financial support package, including $1 billion in new interest-free credits for Nicaragua and Honduras, while some lender countries agreed to forgive all or part of their share of outstanding debt or to delay repayment. Yet with the destruction of much of the infrastructure and export capacity, these nations seem destined to slip further into debt unless there is more debt relief.[54]

In rich and poor nations alike, people living on the margins of society and the economy may be pushed over the edge when disaster strikes. Simply put, disasters make poverty worse. Community and family networks, which provide vital social security, may unravel. For subsistence farmers—both men and women—what little "insurance" they have is in the form of seeds, tools, and livestock, which are often lost along with their crops. Laborers lose their incomes. Traders lose their wares. Squatters or illegal immigrants are usually in high-risk locations to begin with. After disasters, they often do not ask for help because they may fear being evicted from their settlement or deported. Illiterate people cannot read disaster notices and instructions. Those who were homeless before the disaster have no resources or social networks to rely on, and are often invisible to government agencies. Indigenous people often have poor access to information and services before disasters, and are less likely to receive aid afterwards. All in all, the poor and politically powerless are far worse off after disasters.[55]

In Venezuela, the national government's post-landslide reconstruction has emphasized technocratic solutions designed with no input from or consideration of the affected communities. Initial relief efforts focused on road clearing. The long-term master plan is to rebuild Vargas State (the most severely hit) as a posh seaside resort. The government's solution for the poor people of Vargas was to relocate them to rural states in the interior. Eighty percent of those relocated city dwellers are now unemployed and many are returning to Vargas to look for work and rebuild their familial and social networks. Six months after the disaster, 61 percent of those who stayed in Vargas were living in dangerously damaged and severely overcrowded structures, and over half lacked water or sanitation. For those in government shelters, the conditions were even worse. Fed up, the *damnificados* have staged protests and are coordinating their demands for rebuilding jobs, schools, and housing, with an emphasis on self-help projects.[56]

Disasters can weaken the already vulnerable position of women and children. As one flood survivor put it, "life shatters along existing fault lines." Although needs may differ, too many relief efforts fail to make distinctions between men and women. Women may need special medical assistance when pregnant or lactating, or protection from the increased male violence and aggression that commonly occur after disasters. Women usually bear the weight of responsibility for caring for children and the elderly, yet few emergency efforts provide assistance for these tasks. The disproportionate malnourishment of women and children worsens after disasters.[57]

As with development in general, men tend to be seen as the family providers, and relief efforts focus on them to the exclusion of women. "Food for work" jobs and agricultural rebuilding often target men, despite evidence that the food does not always reach the home and is sometimes sold instead, whereas the food and money that a woman works for are almost universally dedicated to her family's needs. Most relief and rebuilding efforts focus on major infrastructure rather than on the priorities of local people, such as affordable housing or income-generating activities.[58]

Finally, planners rarely recognize that in pre- and post-disaster situations, women have different priorities and coping strategies. They generally have less tolerance for risk than men, so they are more likely to prepare for hazards and to heed disaster warnings and evacuation notices. After disasters they are more likely to mobilize social networks to find ways to meet the needs of their family and the community. Men, on the other hand, often cope by leaving the disaster zone to find employment, in some cases abandoning their families.[59]

The tendency to view all disaster victims and their needs alike has a special danger for the disabled and the elderly. In the hurricane-vulnerable coastal communities of North Carolina in the United States, for example, 12 percent of residents have a physical or medical condition that impedes their ability to evacuate their homes—a reality that evacuation plans need to prepare for.[60]

While the "tyranny of the urgent" in disasters makes it easy to overlook social issues, doing so makes efforts far less effective than they need be. Understanding social realities and vulnerabilities is as crucial for ensuring success of all phases of disaster management—from preparedness and response to recovery and mitigation—as it is for achieving truly sustainable development.[61]

The Politics and Psychology of Disasters

Responding to disasters is a genuine human reaction to the suffering of others. When tragedy strikes, there is an almost reflexive outpouring of help to try to feed, clothe, and house those in distress. Yet long-term recovery and disaster prevention efforts rarely elicit the same level of empathy and support. Among donors, governments, and even humanitarian organizations, there is a well-developed culture of response, but not an underlying culture of mitigation. Within the U.S. Office of Foreign Disaster Assistance, for instance, only 11 percent of its meager $155-million 1997 budget went to mitigation and preparedness activities.[62]

When people contemplate the future they "are typically unaware of all the risks and choices they face. They plan only for the immediate future, overestimate their ability to cope when disaster strikes, and rely heavily on emergency relief," according to Dennis Mileti, Director of the Natural Hazards Center and author of *Disasters by Design*. Even when they are aware of risks, people are generally less likely to expend effort and resources on something that might happen, perhaps sometime in the future, than they are to meet more immediate needs. For the very poor, these day-to-day needs are pressing indeed.[63]

While the improved accuracy and dissemination of warnings has saved countless lives, it can, ironically, foster a false sense of safety, and, along with insurance, can encourage people to build and live in risky places. Increasingly sophisticated engineering allows people to wrongly assume that nature can be controlled and thus that they can be completely protected from hazards. In many wealthy countries, such as the United States, most people—rich and poor alike—who choose not to invest in mitigation measures (or even insurance) can do so with a near certain knowledge that they will be physically and financially rescued in the event of an emergency. All this can lead to unnecessary risk taking.

Just as individuals take calculated risks or risks out of ignorance, so too do governments. In many areas of government, including hazard management, short-term thinking prevails. Preparing for and mitigating hazards often take a back seat to other priorities. Rescue and relief get much more financial support—and have more political appeal—than preparing for an event that may not happen during a politician's term in office.

And yet the adage "an ounce of prevention is worth a pound of cure" clearly applies to disasters. The World Bank and U.S. Geological Survey calculated that global economic losses from natural disasters in the 1990s could have been reduced by $280 billion if just one-seventh that amount were invested in preparedness and mitigation efforts. The costs of disaster preparedness and mitigation can be far less than the costs of disaster relief and recovery.[64]

Disasters can focus attention on the many failures in preparation and response. The aftermath of Hurricane Mitch, for instance, brought to light Central America's inadequate disaster preparedness. Despite the fact that the region has been repeatedly hit by hurricanes, earthquakes, and tidal waves, it seems that none of the lessons of those events were learned and applied before Mitch—or since. Nicaragua's government, especially the president, was criticized for failing to declare a state of emergency in the early days of the storm. National emergency planning did not start until days after the storm began, during which time the president repeatedly denied there was a crisis. Early warnings and evacuations could have saved people in the villages around the Las Casitas volcano. After seven days of pounding rains the side of the volcano collapsed into a mile-wide mudslide that buried villages and killed more than 1,400 people—the worst single incident of Mitch.[65]

In Venezuela, there were no national or community disaster preparedness plans or appropriate early warning systems in place when the devastating rains hit in December 1999. Much of the loss of life could have been avoided if such systems had been available, according to a Venezuelan geologist. After the disaster struck, President Chavez, a former Army officer, put the military in charge of response—bypassing state authorities. The months after the disaster were a run-up to elections, and the president and the governor of Vargas State waged a political battle, with the people of Vargas the casualties as relief was delayed. When the governor used relief efforts to bolster his popularity, the president responded by cutting off federal money for disaster assistance. After the president's party won the election, federal help resumed.[66]

In India, the cyclone and tidal wave that hit the desert region of Gujarat and killed 10,000 people in 1998 was predicted by the federal government, but the warnings were not disseminated by local authorities. Some have even said that there was little political will to expend effort warning politically powerless people in the region.[67]

When a supercyclone hit Orissa, India, in late 1999, the official response was decidedly mixed. Though some sectors, such as public health, responded admirably, in general the government's reaction was disjointed and often ineffective. The confusion meant that the people hit hardest by the storm suffered for many days without relief. All told, as many as 50,000 died, 20 million were left homeless, and more than 1 million families lost their means of support. The lack of coastal management plans or an effective emergency communication network also help explains why this cyclone was so destructive compared with similar storms that strike elsewhere. Even a neighboring Indian state was more prepared than Orissa—just a month earlier, Andhra Pradesh managed to evacuate 1 million coastal dwellers to 1,000 cyclone shelters during another storm, while for the supercyclone Orissa evacuated only 150,000 people, and had only 21 shelters for evacuees. Andhra Pradesh had applied the lessons learned in three almost equally large cyclones: in 1974, 10,000 people died in a similar storm; in 1991, 1,000 people died; in 1996, just 60 people were killed.[68]

In Nicaragua, early warnings and evacuations could have saved people in the villages around the Las Casitas volcano.

The failure of governments to develop or enforce adequate land use plans and building codes, even after multiple disasters, can also have devastating consequences. The quake that hit Gujarat, India, in 2001 exposed flaws in construc-

(continued on page 35)

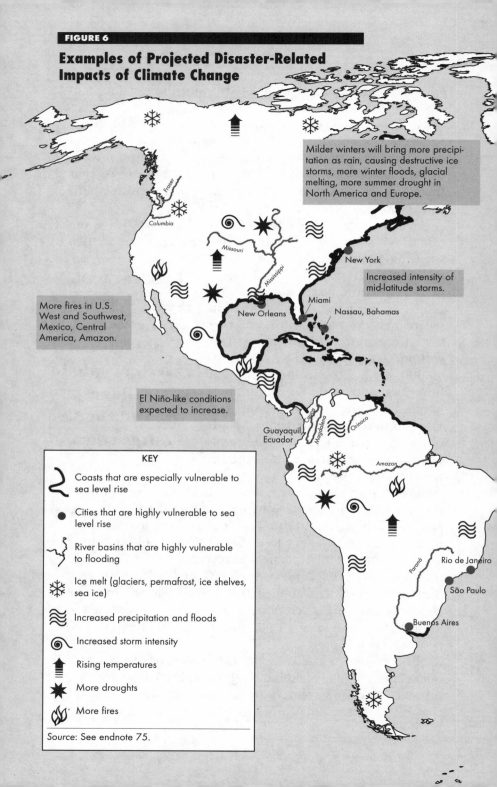

FIGURE 6

Examples of Projected Disaster-Related Impacts of Climate Change

Milder winters will bring more precipitation as rain, causing destructive ice storms, more winter floods, glacial melting, more summer drought in North America and Europe.

Increased intensity of mid-latitude storms.

More fires in U.S. West and Southwest, Mexico, Central America, Amazon.

El Niño-like conditions expected to increase.

Fraser
Columbia
Missouri
Mississippi
New York
Miami
New Orleans
Nassau, Bahamas
Guayaquil, Ecuador
Cauca
Magdalena
Orinoco
Amazon
Paraná
Rio de Janeiro
São Paulo
Buenos Aires

KEY

〰 Coasts that are especially vulnerable to sea level rise

● Cities that are highly vulnerable to sea level rise

〜 River basins that are highly vulnerable to flooding

❄ Ice melt (glaciers, permafrost, ice shelves, sea ice)

≋ Increased precipitation and floods

🌀 Increased storm intensity

⬆ Rising temperatures

✴ More droughts

🔥 More fires

Source: See endnote 75.

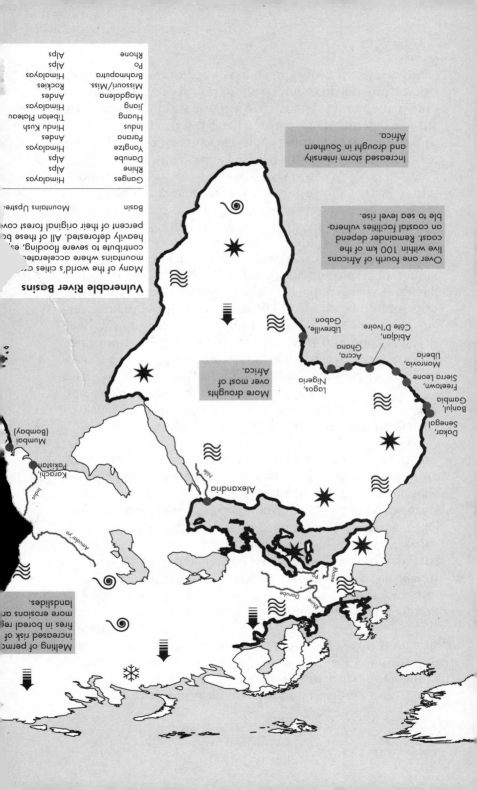

Increased storm intensity and drought in Southern Africa.

Over one fourth of Africans live within 100 km of the coast. Remainder depend on coastal facilities vulnerable to sea level rise.

More droughts over most of Africa.

Melting of perm... increased risk of fires in boreal reg... more erosions ar... landslides.

Vulnerable River Basins

Many of the world's cities ar... mountains where accelerated... contribute to severe flooding, es... heavily deforested. All of these ba... percent of their original forest cov...

Basin	Mountains Upstream
Ganges	Himalayas
Rhine	Alps
Danube	Alps
Yangtze	Himalayas
Parana	Andes
Indus	Hindu Kush
Huang	Tibetan Plateau
Jiang	Himalayas
Magdalena	Andes
Missouri/Miss.	Rockies
Brahmaputra	Himalayas
Po	Alps
Rhone	Alps

Libreville, Gabon
Abidjan, Côte D'Ivoire
Accra, Ghana
Monrovia, Liberia
Lagos, Nigeria
Freetown, Sierra Leone
Banjul, Gambia
Dakar, Senegal
Alexandria
Karachi, Pakistan
Mumbai (Bombay)

Nile
Amudar'ya
Indus
Po
Rhone
Danube
Rhine

es blowing away but from massive water damage due to bro-ken roofs or windows that had been constructed in violation of building codes.) For communities that lack the technical expertise to develop their own, model codes and standards can provide guidance.[71]

Ineffective development and enforcement of building codes are not the only governance problems faced by hazard-prone communities. According to the *World Disasters Report*: "Corruption and vested interests in and around government play a large role in many of the long-term precursors to dis-aster. Mafia organizations have been implicated in the wide-spread construction of illegal housing in disaster-prone areas of Italy. Timber smuggling cartels with political connections on the porous borders of Pakistan and Afghanistan are denuding and destabilizing mountain slopes in earthquake zones."[72]

In Indonesia, not only did former president Suharto's government turn a blind eye to timber and palm oil planta-tion owners (many of whom were his cronies) who were ille-gally using fire to clear forest to expand their operations, but some of the 1997–98 fires were set as part of the govern-ment's own misguided program to turn 1 million hectares of peat swamp into an agricultural settlement. Early on, the government tried to blame the rural poor for setting the fires that swept the country, despite satellite images tracing almost all the blazes to corporate plantations and timber concessions. When the government finally admitted who the real culprits were, little or nothing was done to stop them. Nor was anything done to help the millions who lost their homes and livelihoods or were sickened by the haze, while the nongovernmental organizations (NGOs) that stepped in to provide services were criticized.[73]

Governments should beware, as the failure to prepare for and respond to disasters can have political repercussions. In Indonesia, Suharto was finally ousted when outrage over the Asian financial crisis and the massive fires fanned the flames of widespread opposition to the regime's corrupt and author-itarian rule. And in the elections following the Orissa disas-

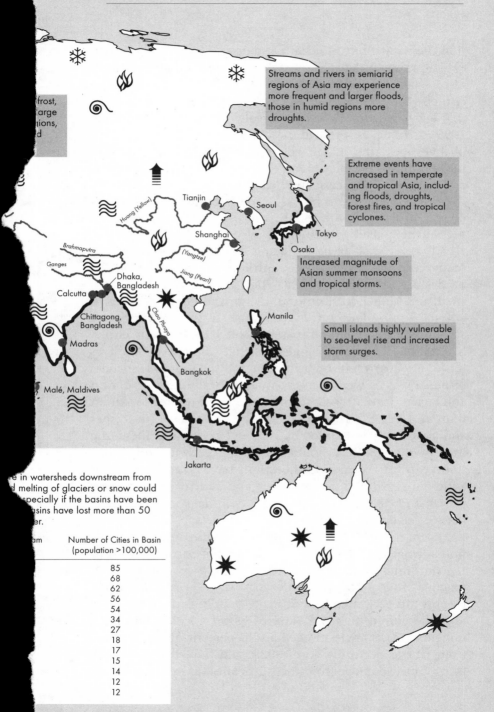

Streams and rivers in semiarid regions of Asia may experience more frequent and larger floods, those in humid regions more droughts.

Extreme events have increased in temperate and tropical Asia, including floods, droughts, forest fires, and tropical cyclones.

Increased magnitude of Asian summer monsoons and tropical storms.

Small islands highly vulnerable to sea-level rise and increased storm surges.

frost,
arge
ions,
d

Huang (Yellow)

Tianjin

Seoul

Shanghai

(Yangtze)

Tokyo

Osaka

Jiang (Pearl)

Brahmaputra

Ganges

Dhaka, Bangladesh

Calcutta

Chittagong, Bangladesh

Madras

Chao Phaya

Manila

Bangkok

Malé, Maldives

Jakarta

e in watersheds downstream from
d melting of glaciers or snow could
pecially if the basins have been
asins have lost more than 50
er.

am	Number of Cities in Basin (population >100,000)
	85
	68
	62
	56
	54
	34
	27
	18
	17
	15
	14
	12
	12

tion that contributed to death and destruction. And in earth-quake-prone Turkey, as elsewhere, rapid urbanization in recent decades led to a housing crisis. To alleviate the crunch, 15 "building amnesties" were granted since 1950 that legalized what had been illegal construction. Before the 1999 earthquakes, these amnesties were seen as a great populist gesture. After the quakes and nearly 18,000 deaths, corrupt building contractors and local officials were denounced as "murderers" in newspaper headlines. While many poorly constructed apartment blocks, some as far away as 100 kilometers, turned into tombs, other properly constructed buildings at the quake's epicenter survived.[69]

Turkey is not alone in facing this type of problem. In many cities in developing countries, more than half of all homes are technically illegal. They are poorly constructed, sited, and served. In Honduras, the government has failed to enforce zoning laws introduced after Hurricane Mitch. Not all poorly located buildings are inhabited by the poor, either. In Venezuela, the 1999 landslides that claimed 30,000 lives hit luxury apartment high-rises built at the foot of landslide-prone slopes as well as more modest dwellings. Corruption and lack of regulations had allowed a building free-for-all. In Bhuj and other cities of Gujarat, the earthquake hit homes and apartments inhabited by rich and poor alike, including newer buildings that should have been constructed to withstand earthquakes. Serious questions have been raised about adherence to building standards and lack of enforcement power, and claims of homicide and criminal conspiracy have been leveled against builders and architects.[70]

Even in the industrial world, building in risky locations—from the cliffs of California to the barrier islands of the Carolinas and the mountains of Italy—is a widespread practice and problem. Sometimes it is even subsidized. Hazard mitigation codes can make buildings safer, but they must be enforced. If the State of Florida's codes had been upheld, for instance, more than 25 percent of the damage from Hurricane Andrew in 1992 could have been avoided. (Most of the damage from the hurricane was not from hous-

ter in India, the incumbent party was ousted by voters angry over the government's apathy, bungling, and corruption.[74]

Fostering Resilience in Nature and Communities

The ever-rising human and economic toll of disasters provides clear evidence that a shift is needed in our coping strategies. This shift is all the more urgent if the current trends that make us vulnerable continue: the concentration of people and infrastructure in cities and along coasts, as well as growing pressure on ecosystems. The looming prospect of climate change and sea level rise can only exacerbate these troubling trends.

Scientists project that in the future the weather is likely to become more erratic and extreme as a result of climate change. The Intergovernmental Panel on Climate Change (IPCC) reports that the globally averaged surface air temperature is projected to increase 1.4–5.8 degrees Celsius by 2100 relative to 1990. New IPCC studies highlight the projected disaster-related impacts of climate change during the twenty-first century. These include increased coastal flooding and infrastructure damage due to sea level rise; higher maximum temperatures with more droughts, heat waves, and fires in many areas; more intense tropical storms; more intense precipitation events over most regions that will increase floods, landslides, avalanches, and mudslides; and intensified droughts and floods associated with El Niño events. The IPCC projects that "the most widespread risk to settlements from climate change is flooding and landslides driven by projected increases in rainfall intensity and, in coastal areas, sea level rise." In Asia, projections of sea level rise, increased floods and droughts in both temperate and tropical areas, and heavier monsoon rains will worsen the problems of this densely populated and disaster-prone region. (See Figure 6, pages 32–34.)[75]

It is already clear that sea levels are rising. During the twentieth century, global average sea level rose by 10–20 centimeters, according to the IPCC, and it is projected to rise another 9–88 centimeters by 2100. But some areas will likely experience sea level increases of twice the global average, notes the British Meteorological Office. The IPCC projects that the average number of people who would be flooded by coastal storm surges would increase severalfold, meaning some 75–200 million more people would be affected every year, even under a mid-range increase in sea level.[76]

Coastal cities, river deltas, and small islands will be especially vulnerable. Major river deltas like Bangladesh, the Amazon, the Mekong, the Mississippi, the Nile, and others would be at risk. Some small island nations may see their national territory disappear. Rising sea levels could even flood the New York City subway system and turn parts of the metropolitan area into wetlands. Some of the most heavily populated and disaster-prone areas of Asia, such as Bangladesh, Indonesia, and Viet Nam, are projected to lose substantial portions of their land to sea level rise, with tens of millions of people directly affected, according to IPCC estimates. (See Table 1.) The IPCC emphasizes that "the impacts of future changes in climate extremes are expected to fall disproportionately on the poor."[77]

Some of the costs of climate change have already been felt, and they are projected to increase in the future. All told, the direct economic costs of climate change worldwide could top $300 billion per year, according to Munich Re and the U.N. Environment Programme. Individual nations could experience tens of billions of dollars in damage to coastal infrastructure from sea level rise, notes the IPCC. The IPCC reports that evidence of climate change has already been observed in Asia, and that signs will become even more obvious in the next 10–20 years. The scientists' panel warns that "if this time is not used to design and implement adaptations, it may be too late to avoid more upheaval," and that such adaptations in Asia and elsewhere will be needed even if future greenhouse gas emissions are reduced.[78]

TABLE 1

Potential Land Loss and Population Exposed by Sea Level Rise, Selected Countries

Country	Potential Land Loss		Population Exposed	
	(square kilometers)	(percent)	(million)	(percent)
Africa				
Egypt	2,000	<1	8	11.7
Senegal	6,000	3.1	0.2	2.3
Nigeria	600	<1	>3.7	3
Tanzania	2,117	<1		
Americas				
Belize	1,900	8.4	0.07	35
Guyana			0.6	80
Venezuela	5,700	0.6	0.06	<1
North America	19,000	<1	—	—
Asia				
Bangladesh	29,846	20.7	14.8	13.5
India	5,763	0.4	7.1	0.8
Indonesia	34,000	1.9	2.0	1.1
Japan	1,412	0.4	2.9	2.3
Malaysia	7,000	2.1	>0.05	>0.3
Viet Nam	40,000	12.1	17.1	23.1
Europe				
Netherlands	2,165	6.7	10	67
Germany	—	—	3.1	4

Note: Estimates based on 1-meter rise except for 0.5 meters in North America and Japan and 0.6 meters in Indonesia.
Source: See endnote 77.

There is ample opportunity for actions to reduce disaster risks within the Framework Convention on Climate Change, as there is language that obliges signatories to cooperate in adapting to the impacts of climate change, including land use and water resource planning as well as disaster mitigation. The value of incorporating disaster mitigation and adaptation to climate change into efforts to achieve sustainable and equitable development is highlighted in the latest IPCC reports. The "win-win" solutions are summed up: "Policies that lessen pressures on resources, improve management of environmental risks, and increase the welfare of the poorest members of society can simultaneously advance sustainable development and equity, enhance adaptive capacity, and reduce vulnerability to climate and other stresses."[79]

Too often, uncertainties over "the weather" or "the climate" are used as excuses for inaction. But it is important to recognize that irrespective of any potential climate change dimension, we continue to put more people and more "stuff"—buildings, bridges, cities, and power plants—in harm's way and have weakened nature's ability to mitigate hazards. Equally important is understanding that just as our development choices have made the threats worse, we have the power to make better choices.

There is a growing awareness that disaster response and recovery—the traditional mainstays of past efforts—are not enough, and that mitigation actions are needed to reduce the impacts of natural disasters. The need for a new direction in policies toward disasters is evident in the rising costs of these events to government treasuries. In the United States, for example, between 1970 and 1981 domestic disaster assistance cost the federal government $3.8 billion. But for 1989–94, a period half as long, the bill topped $34 billion.[80]

While we cannot do away with natural hazards, we can eliminate those that we cause, minimize those we exacerbate, and reduce our vulnerability to most. Doing this requires healthy and resilient communities and ecosystems. Viewed in this light, disaster mitigation is clearly part of a broader strategy of sustainable development—making communities and nations socially, economically, and ecologically sustainable.

How can communities and nations begin to mitigate disasters and reduce the human and economic toll? They can make sure that they understand their risks and vulnerabilities. They can use this knowledge to ensure that their development efforts do not inadvertently increase the likelihood and severity of disasters. To the extent possible, people and structures should be located out of harm's way. When hazards are unavoidable, development can be made to withstand them—for example, buildings in earthquake zones should be designed to weather earthquakes. Disaster preparedness, too, is an integral part of saving lives and lowering the economic toll. And every segment of the community needs to be actively engaged in planning and implementing disaster mitigation efforts.

Identifying and delineating natural resources (like watersheds and floodplains), hazards (such as flood zones), vulnerable infrastructure (such as buildings, power lines, and bridges), as well as vulnerable communities and resources—and doing so at scales that are meaningful to communities and decisionmakers—is an essential step. Yet hazard mapping is incomplete, outdated, or non-existent in many communities and nations. Even most U.S. flood maps are more than 20 years old, and most other hazards are not mapped at all. Maps do not show the areas that would be flooded in the event of a dam or levee failure, or that are at risk from coastal

In the next 60 years, 25 percent of homes within 500 feet of U.S. shorelines are projected to be lost to coastal erosion.

erosion—despite the fact that in the next 60 years, 25 percent of homes within 500 feet of U.S. shorelines are projected to be lost to coastal erosion.[81]

A critical part of good land use planning is maintaining or restoring healthy ecosystems so they can provide valuable services. China, for example, now recognizes that forests are 10 times more valuable for flood control and water supply than they are for timber. Since the logging ban was introduced, the government has been paying former loggers to plant trees in the upper watershed. The resiliency of agroecological farming practices in the face of Hurricane Mitch, noted earlier, provides a model for better land use.[82]

Ecosystem restoration and rehabilitation can be effective tools in hazard mitigation. An extensive study by the U.S. National Research Council recommended these tools to solve water quality, wildlife, and flooding problems at minimal cost and disruption. Restoring half of the wetlands lost in the upper Mississippi Basin would affect less than 3 percent of the agricultural, forest, or urban land, yet it could prevent a repeat of the flood that drowned the heartland in 1993. Allowing more of the natural floodplain to function can reduce the impact of future floods on human settlements and economic activities. Similarly, in the United Kingdom, substantial portions of forest and wetland habitat have been lost, and 10 percent of the population lives in flood-prone areas. A proposal has been made to expand the government's habitat restoration targets to provide local flood protection and wildlife benefits. The autumn floods of 2000 are a stark reminder of how much those flood protection services are needed.[83]

Restoration has benefits beyond hazard mitigation. In Viet Nam, 2,000 hectares of mangroves were planted to act as a buffer against frequent coastal storms and to provide local livelihood benefits by boosting production of a range of mangrove-dependent sea products like shrimp, fish, and seaweed. The restoration effort has proved successful on both counts. When the area was hit by the worst typhoon in a decade, there was no significant damage.[84]

Restoring the native vegetation of South Africa by eliminating invasive species is essential for reducing the risk of dangerous fires, improving water availability, and protecting the most globally unique center of biodiversity—the Cape Floral Kingdom. "Ukuvuka: Operation Firestop Campaign" is a public-private partnership that aims to do just that. And in the process, Ukuvuka—meaning "to wake up" in the Xhosa language—is creating much-needed employment and benefits for South Africa's disadvantaged communities, who clear the invasives and make secondary products from the wood. One of its government partners, the Working for Water Programme of the Department of Water Affairs and Forestry, is a nationwide effort. (Generating current benefits like employment is a vital element for mitigation strategies in many countries where meeting people's pressing day-to-day needs is a top priority.) Preventing the fires also helps protect the inhabitants of the vast Apartheid-era settlements, which have minimal access to fire brigades. In South Africa, national laws have also been enacted that oblige private landowners to control invasive species on their property.[85]

In the past, making communities safe was seen as the job of engineers, who, for instance, would apply structural solutions to flood control and coastal storms—a costly and often unsuccessful approach. As noted earlier, many of these structures have ironically contributed to a false sense of security and to magnifying the hazard. Many of them are now reaching the end of their life span and should be decommissioned.

The time has come to tap nature's engineering techniques.

Instead of relying on structural engineering, the time has come to tap nature's engineering techniques—using the services provided by healthy and resilient ecosystems. Dunes, barrier islands, mangrove forests, and coastal wetlands are natural shock absorbers that protect against coastal storms. Wetlands, floodplains, and forests are sponges that absorb floodwaters. Nature provides these valuable services for free, and we should take advantage of them rather than undermining them.

There is still a role for traditional engineering. Buildings and bridges can be made to better withstand natural hazards. By ensuring that structures can withstand earthquakes of a certain magnitude, or winds of a certain speed, many lives and dollars could be saved. Better engineering and enforcement of residential and commercial building codes is the major reason why an earthquake in Japan or the United States is so much less deadly than one in the developing world.[86]

Making communities safer does not have to be high tech

or high cost. In Maharastra, India, "barefoot" engineers and builders helped introduce new and safer building techniques during post-earthquake reconstruction. In many flood-adapted cultures—like in the Amazon or Mekong—houses sit on stilts above the high water mark or float up and down with the water levels. In Bangladesh, communities build and maintain raised mounds where they can go for safety during floods. The mound usually has a safe drinking-water well and a school or other community structure, providing a safe haven and an incentive for the community to maintain it. Active community participation in planning and implementation of all levels of disaster mitigation and recovery is essential.[87]

Basic community services have added benefits during disasters. As noted earlier, China credits improved sanitation with virtually eliminating the post-disaster epidemics of waterborne diseases that frequently used to kill more people than the disaster itself.

Communities can also act to reduce the "hidden hazards" that can create a "disaster after the disaster." After Hurricane Floyd hit North Carolina in 1999, for example, the contents of open waste ponds of industrial hog farms spread out over the landscape in the floodwaters. Chemical plants and other industrial sites also present special hazards during natural disasters. Ensuring safe containment of these facilities can save many lives and considerable money in post-disaster cleanup efforts. Among the most frightening and deadly hidden hazards are the land mines that are washed by floodwaters to new and unmapped locations, as has happened in Mozambique, Central America, and Bosnia Herzegovina.[88]

In recent decades, great strides have been made in predicting extreme weather events and disseminating warnings. In 1992, warnings and timely evacuations were a major factor in limiting to 15 the number of deaths caused by Andrew, the costliest hurricane in U.S. history (at $30 billion). A comprehensive preparedness system has helped reduce the loss of life in Bangladesh, 90 percent of which is vulnerable to cyclones. Tens of thousands of community volunteers, working in teams of 10 men and 2 women, provide warnings, evacuation, search and rescue, and other emergency assistance—often at risk to their own lives. They are credited with saving 30,000 people in the powerful 1991 cyclone and countless others in recent events.[89]

Getting the right information to the right people at the right time remains an enormous challenge. Sometimes information is too technical to be useful or is in the wrong language. Radio, television, satellites, computers, and the Internet can be very effective in expanding dissemination, yet much of the world—including most of Africa—is still without access to many of these technologies. Expanding effective early warning systems should continue to be a high priority.[90]

Sustainable mitigation must be an integral part of local and international development plans. Governments have a role to play in investing in hazard and risk assessments and in developing databases on losses, mitigation efforts, and social data. They can establish land use policies, limit subsidization of risk and destructive activities, use incentives to encourage sound land use and sustainable hazard mitigation, and encourage collaboration between agencies and civil society.[91]

Governments and civil society must also ensure the rule of law—without it, the social and ecological unraveling that precipitates and exacerbates disasters is far more likely. The fires in Indonesia provide a textbook case on the consequences of corruption and lawlessness. Russia may be unwittingly setting the stage for future disasters by allowing massive and poorly regulated logging in its Far East. Since China enacted its much needed logging ban in 1998 to restore the health of the flood-ravaged Yangtze basin, the impacts of logging have shifted to neighboring countries like Russia and elsewhere.[92]

Private and public insurers can help reduce hazard losses by providing information and education as well as incentives that encourage mitigation and disincentives to discourage building in hazard-prone places. Insurers have been active and constructive participants in the climate change debate, as they recognize the huge potential impacts of climate change on their industry. For most of the developing world, insurance is not available. Providing some sort of financial safety net is a large and unmet need.[93]

The publicly funded U.S. National Flood Insurance Program provides insurance in communities that adopt a set of minimum standards for floodplain management. Reduced insurance premiums are provided for communities that undertake activities (such as flood mapping, preparedness, public information, and so forth) that exceed minimum standards. While there have been some changes in the program, much more could be done. Currently, because erosion hazards are not mapped, homeowners in erosion-prone areas pay the same flood insurance rates as those in no-risk areas. The NFIP also reimburses communities for "beach nourishment": the costly, futile, and potentially destructive practice of regularly plowing sand from the ocean up to the beach. In the future, NFIP rates could be raised and coupled with land use controls such as mandatory setbacks from hazardous zones.[94]

Donors can provide leverage and resources to promote development policies that include disaster mitigation. As noted, a dollar spent on disaster preparedness can prevent $7 in disaster-related economic losses—a great return on investment. Considering the social and ecological losses that are also prevented, the return is far higher.[95]

Unfortunately, overall foreign aid budgets are small, and disaster prevention allocations are minuscule. At the 1992 Earth Summit, the Group of Seven industrial countries made a commitment to provide 0.7 percent of their GDP in overseas development assistance, yet seven years later they had managed to come up with only 0.39 percent. Of the aid that they do provide, what is spent for emergency assistance is painfully small. In 1997 it was less than 7 percent of bilateral aid. The amount spent for mitigation was far lower.[96]

Efforts to restore people's livelihoods and help the poorest of the poor are also shortchanged. Too often aid neglects people in favor of buildings. A survey reported in the latest *World Disasters Report* found that 53 percent of post-disaster aid projects were for infrastructure, while only 10 percent were for economic recovery. And far too much of the money for these projects is paid to contractors from the donor countries, a practice that deprives "recipient" nations of much needed local economic benefits. Also troubling is that the share of bilateral relief going to the poorest countries—those hardest hit and with the least resources—fell from 46 percent in 1995 to 28 percent in 1999.[97]

A dollar spent on disaster preparedness can prevent $7 in disaster-related economic losses.

Better coordination of emergency and development efforts within and among agencies is needed. In the United Nations, for instance, weather forecasting, humanitarian relief, food relief, and disaster preparedness and mitigation are each in separate agencies. Some donors are beginning to integrate these functions, a step that can help mainstream mitigation. The World Bank recently launched the ProVention consortium, in partnership with governments, intergovernmental organizations, private insurance companies, universities, and NGOs. Yet within the Bank, disaster and development are still largely segregated, and neither seems to influence the onerous debt demands of the World Bank, the International Monetary Fund (IMF), and other lenders on disaster-stricken countries.[98]

Donors and lenders also have the opportunity—and the obligation—to resolve the debt burden that cripples many nations. The huge amount of money needed for both immediate disaster relief and long-term reconstruction in Central America after Hurricane Mitch and in Mozambique after Cyclone Eline focused attention on the growing problem of debt. Many question how these nations can realistically be expected to provide for their citizens and rebuild while repaying mounting foreign debt, especially since much of their capacity to generate revenue was wiped out by the storm. Before Mitch, Honduras owed $4.7 billion in external debt and Nicaragua owed $5.7 billion. In Nicaragua, per capita GDP was less than $400, while even before the hurricane, each person's share of foreign debt was nearly three times that.[99]

A few months after floods and cyclones ravaged Mozambique, affecting nearly 5 million people, donor nations pledged $453 billion to fully fund its reconstruction. While Mozambique has received some measure of debt relief, debt elimination is what is needed. The massive floods that hit the nation anew in 2001 were a drenching reminder.[100]

Much of the heralded post-Mitch "debt relief" involves simply postponing payments and supplying more loans (and therefore debt). The skepticism that met most creditor initiatives was summed up by the Roman Catholic Archbishop of Tegucigalpa, Oscar Andres Rodriguez, who likened the lender's moratorium on debt repayment to a "stay of execution." The devastation wrought by back-to-back earthquakes early in 2001 underscores the severity of the ultimate debt sentence.[101]

Indeed, the debt and the structural adjustment and austerity programs of recent decades have forced extreme cutbacks in social services, such as health care and education, and in environmental and resource management programs—precisely the kinds of services that are needed to help prevent disasters and respond effectively when they occur. The new loans and adjustment programs are accelerating these cutbacks. One year after Hurricane Mitch, Nicaragua had spent almost as much on debt service ($170 million) as on reconstruction ($190 million). The IMF explicitly stated that Nicaragua must limit reconstruction spending to $190 million per year in 1999 and 2000.[102]

What Central America needs for reconstruction, said Archbishop Rodriguez, "is debt cancellation, combined with adequate foreign assistance and with careful oversight by our civil society," an approach championed by the faith-based Jubilee 2000 coalition that applies equally as well in many disaster-stricken nations. Oxfam has proposed that no more than 10 percent of government revenues could be spent on debt payments. Such limits are not without precedent. After World War II, Germany's debt payments were limited to 3.5 percent of export revenues in order to spur peace and development. Yet today the IMF, World Bank, and the Paris Club of government creditors say that 20–25 percent is sustainable, a level far higher than industrial nations deemed sustainable for themselves in the past.[103]

The International Decade for Natural Disaster Reduction that ended in 1999 represented an important opportunity to raise the profile of hazards and disasters, advance science and policy, and inspire national action. Yet it may have been "a decade of missed opportunity," in the words of eminent geographer Gilbert White, as it focused on scientific and technical programs but failed to strengthen local capacity or to address slow-onset events such as those that plague Africa, among other important aspects of disaster reduction. To continue and expand the efforts of the decade, the United Nations has established a follow-up process, the International Strategy for Disaster Reduction. Unfortunately, it has relatively little visibility or political muscle, despite the tremendous challenges ahead.[104]

The international community has additional avenues for action. As discussed earlier, the Framework Convention on Climate Change provides the rationale for bringing together the goals of adapting to climate change, mitigating disasters, and fostering equitable and sustainable development. The parties to the convention have agreed to establish a fund to help developing countries finance such adaptation.[105]

Many have concluded that the time has come for a profound shift in how we approach disasters. As Kunda Dixit and Inam Ahmed put it, when writing about floods in the vast Himalayan watershed: "Complete flood control... is impossible. Even partial control is... problematic.... So the question arises: Should we try to prevent floods at all? Or should we be looking at what it is we do that makes floods worse? Is it better to try to live with them, and to minimize the danger to infrastructure while maximizing the advantages that annual floods bring to farmers?" The same questions must be asked about natural hazards everywhere.[106]

If we continue on a course of undermining the health and resilience of nature, putting ourselves in harm's way, and delaying mitigation measures, we set ourselves up for more unnatural disasters, more suffering, more economic losses, and more delayed development. If instead we choose to work with nature and each other, we can reduce the waves of unnatural disasters that have been washing over the shores of humanity with increasing regularity and ferocity.

Notes

1. International Federation of Red Cross and Red Crescent Societies (Red Cross), *World Disasters Report 2001* (Geneva: 2001), pp. 83–101; Howard LaFranchi, "After the Flood: Hope in Venezuela," *Christian Science Monitor*, 2 June 2000.

2. U.S. Department of State, Bureau of Western Hemisphere Affairs, "Background Notes: Honduras," October 1999, <www.state.gov/www/ background_notes/honduras_1099_bgn.html>, viewed 23 August 2000; gross domestic product from World Bank, *World Development Indicators 1999* (Washington, DC: 1999); Christian Aid, "In Debt to Disaster: What Happened to Honduras after Hurricane Mitch," October 1999, <www. christian-aid.org.uk/reports/indebt/indebt2.html>, viewed 22 August 2000.

3. Economic losses from Munich Reinsurance Company (Munich Re), *Topics: Annual Review of Natural Catastrophes 1999* (Munich: June 2000).

4. Death toll in 1998–99 from ibid., and from Munich Re, *Topics: Annual Review of Natural Catastrophes 1998* (Munich: March 1999); Gujarat from ibid.; Orissa from "Catastrophe!" *Down to Earth*, 30 November 1999; Indonesia from Charles Victor Barber and James Schweithelm, *Trial by Fire: Forest Fires and Forestry Policy in Indonesia's Era of Crisis and Reform* (Washington, DC: World Resources Institute, World Wide Fund for Nature–Indonesia, and Telepak Indonesia Foundation, 2000), p. 10; fires from Andy Rowell and Dr. Peter F. Moore, "Global Review of Forest Fires," Metis Associates for World Wide Fund for Nature and IUCN–World Conservation Union, 1999, <www.panda.org/forests4life/fires/fire_ report.doc>, viewed 27 July 2000; Venezuela from Red Cross, op. cit. note 1, p. 83.

5. Munich Re, "Gujarat (India) Earthquake of 26.1.2001" MRNatCat Poster #15; "Post-Mitch Reconstruction Destroyed by El Salvador Earthquake," *Yahoo News*, 16 January 2001; Mozambique from Red Cross, "Mozambique: Flood Relief and Rehabilitation," Appeal No. 10/2001, 3 July 2001.

6. Deforestation from World Resources Institute, *World Resources 2000–2001* (Washington, DC: 2000), pp. 252–55; land and population distribution from World Neighbors, *Reasons for Resiliency: Toward a Sustainable Recovery after Hurricane Mitch* (Tegucigalpa, Honduras: 2000), p. 8.

7. Recovery cost savings from John Twigg, ed., *Developments at Risk: Natural Disasters and the Third World* (Oxford, U.K.: Oxford Centre for Disaster Studies, UK Coordinated Committee for the IDNDR, May 1998).

8. Munich Re, *World Map of Natural Hazards* (Munich: 1998), p. 19.

9. Figure 1 from Munich Re, op. cit. note 3, p. 19.

10. Munich Re, *Topics: Annual Review: Natural Catastrophes 2000* (Munich: 2001), p. 2.

11. Figure 2 and 3 from Munich Re, *Topics 2000: Natural Catastrophes—The Current Position* (Munich: December 1999), pp. 64–65.

12. Munich Re, op. cit. note 11; homeless from Worldwatch analysis of data from the Centre for Research on the Epidemiology of Disasters (CRED), EM-DAT Database (Brussels, Belgium), <www.md.ucl.ac.be/cred/emdat/intro.html>, obtained June 2000.

13. Munich Re, op. cit. note 11, p. 123.

14. China from Red Cross, *World Disasters Report 1999* (Geneva: 1999), p. 34; increased diseases from James J. McCarthy et al., eds., *Climate Change 2001: Impacts, Adaptation, and Vulnerability: Contribution of Working Group II to the Third Assessment of the Intergovernmental Panel on Climate Change* (Cambridge, U.K.: Cambridge University Press, 2001), pp. 12, 719; "Up to One Third of Malaria Deaths in Africa Occur in Countries Affected by Complex Emergencies," *Bulletin of the World Health Organization*, vol. 78, no. 8 (2000).

15. Red Cross, op. cit. note 1, Table 13.

16. Deaths and economic losses from Munich Re, op. cit. note 11; homeless from CRED, op. cit. note 12; China from Vaclav Smil and Mao Yushi, coord., *The Economic Costs of China's Environmental Degradation* (Cambridge, MA: American Academy of Arts and Sciences, 1998), p. 35; Rhine from "Dyke Disaster," *Down to Earth*, 15 March 1995.

17. Munich Re, op. cit. note 3, p. 19; Kobe from Munich Re, op. cit. note 11, p. 14; Seth Dunn, "Weather-Related Losses Hit New High," in Lester R. Brown, Michael Renner, and Brian Halweil, *Vital Signs 1999* (New York: W.W. Norton & Company), pp. 74–75, based on data from Munich Re; Gerhard Berz, "Insuring Against Catastrophe," *Our Planet* (U.N. Environment Programme), vol. 11, no. 3 (2001), pp. 19–20.

18. Red Cross, op. cit. note 1, p. 163.

19. Figure 4 from Munich Re, op. cit. note 11, pp. 64–65.

20. Figure 5 from Munich Re, op. cit. note 3, p. 24. "Richest countries" are defined as having a per capita annual gross domestic product greater than $9,361, while "poorest" are defined as those with less than $760.

21. Peter B. Bayley, "Understanding Large River-Floodplain Ecosystems," *Bioscience*, March 1995, pp. 153–58; J.V. Ward and J.A. Stanford, "Riverine Ecosystems: The Influence of Man on Catchment Dynamics and Fish Ecology," in D.P. Dodge, ed., *Proceedings of the International Large River*

Symposium, Canadian Special Publication of Fisheries and Aquatic Sciences 106 (Ottawa: Department of Fisheries and Oceans, 1989), pp. 56–64; Kunda Dixit and Inam Ahmed, "Managing the Himalayan Watershed: A Flood of Questions," *Economic and Political Weekly*, 31 October 1998, p. 2772.

22. "Summary for Policymakers," in McCarthy et al., op. cit. note 14, p. 14; Red Cross, op. cit. note 1, Table 6.

23. "Flood Impact on Economy Limited—Expert," *China Daily*, 1 September 1998; Red Cross, "China: Floods, Appeal no 21/98 (Revised)," 9 November 1998; Yangtze deforestation from Carmen Revenga et al., *Watersheds of the World* (Washington, DC: World Resources Institute and Worldwatch Institute, 1998).

24. Erik Eckholm, "China Admits Ecological Sins Played Role in Flood Disaster," *New York Times*, 26 August 1998; John Pomfret, "Yangtze Flood Jolts China's Land Policies," *Washington Post*, 22 November 1998.

25. Eckholm, op. cit. note 24; Indira A. R. Lakshaman, "China Says Policies Worsened Floods, Beijing Alleges Corruption by Local Aides," *Boston Globe*, 17 August 1998; "China Flood: Logging Ban Announced to Check Devastating Floods," *Agence France Presse*, 23 August 1998; Erik Eckholm, "Stunned by Floods, China Hastens Logging Curbs," *New York Times*, 27 September 1998; Peichang Zhang et al., "China's Forest Policy for the 21st Century," *Science*, 23 June 2000, pp. 2135–36.

26. William Weaver and Danny K. Hagans, "Aerial Reconnaissance Evaluation of 1996 Storm Effects on Upland Mountainous Watersheds of Oregon and Southern Washington: Wildland Response to the February 1996 Storm and Flood in the Oregon and Washington Cascades and Oregon Coast Range Mountains," paper prepared for Pacific Rivers Council, Eugene, OR (Arcata, CA: Pacific Watershed Associates, May 1996); "A Tale of Two Cities—and Their Drinking Water," in Sierra Club, *Stewardship or Stumps? National Forests at the Crossroads* (Washington, DC: June 1997); Romain Cooper, "Floods in the Forest," *Headwaters Forest News*, spring 1997; David Bayles, "Logging and Landslides," *New York Times*, 19 February 1997; William Claiborne, "When a Verdant Forest Turns Ugly: 8 Oregon Deaths Blamed on Mud Sliding Down Clear-Cut Hillsides," *Washington Post*, 18 December 1996.

27. Brazil fires and ecology from Daniel C. Nepstad et al., "Large-Scale Impoverishment of Amazonian Forests by Logging and Fire," *Nature*, 8 April 1999, pp. 505–08; Indonesia from BAPPENAS (National Development Planning Agency), 1999, cited in Barber and Schweithelm, op. cit. note 4; Rowell and Moore, op. cit. note 4.

28. BAPPENAS, op. cit. note 27.

29. Barber and Schweithelm, op. cit. note 4.

30. *The Cape of Flames: The Great Fire of January 2000* (Kenilworth, South Africa: Inyati Publishing, The Cape Argus, and the Santam/Cape Argus Ukuvuku, December 2000); Working for Water Programme, <www-dwaf.pwv.gov.za/wfw>; affected area and water flow from D.B. Versfeld et al., *Alien Invading Plants and Water Resources in South Africa: A Preliminary Assessment* (Pretoria: Water Research Commission, 1998), Foreword and p. ii.

31. U.S. Department of Agriculture, Forest Service, "Managing the Impact of Wildfires on Communities and the Environment: A Report to the President in Response to the Wildfires of 2000" (Washington, DC: 8 September 2000); Paul Duggan, "Wildfires Engulf Thousands of Western Acres," *Washington Post*, 26 July 2000; Douglas Jehl, "Population Shift in the West Raises Wildfire Concerns: Los Alamos a Reminder," *New York Times*, 30 May 2000; Christopher J. Huggard and Arthur R. Gomez, eds., *Forests under Fire: A Century of Ecosystem Mismanagement in the Southwest* (Tucson: University of Arizona Press, 2001); Kurt Kleiner, "Fanning the Wildfires," *New Scientist*, 19 October 1996; fire statistics and costs from National Interagency Fire Center, "Wildland Fire Statistics" <www.nifc.gov/stats/wildlandfirestats.html>, viewed 16 July 2001.

32. Effects of flood control devices from Edward Goldsmith and Nicholas Hildyard, *The Social and Environmental Effects of Large Dams, Vol. One: Overview* (Camelford, Cornwall, U.K.: Wadebridge Ecological Centre, 1984); Munich Re, op. cit. note 10, pp. 31–32; Rhine from Haig Simonian, "Flood of Tears on the Rhine," *Financial Times*, 8 February 1995; historic flood data from "Dyke Disaster," op. cit. note 16.

33. Impacts from Gerald E. Galloway, "The Mississippi Basin Flood of 1993," prepared for Workshop on Reducing the Vulnerability of River Basin Energy, Agriculture and Transportation Systems to Floods, Foz do Iguacu, Brazil, 29 November 1995, from Stanley A. Changnon, ed., *The Great Flood of 1993: Causes, Impacts and Responses* (Boulder, CO: Westview Press, 1996), from James M. Wright, *The Nation's Responses to Flood Disasters: A Historical Account* (Madison, WI: Association of State Floodplain Managers, Inc. (ASFPM), April 2000), and from Donald L. Hey and Nancy S. Philippi, "Flood Reduction through Wetland Restoration: The Upper Mississippi River Basin as a Case History," *Restoration Ecology*, March 1995, pp. 4–17; costs from Committee on Assessing the Costs of Natural Disasters, *The Impacts of Natural Disasters* (Washington, DC: National Academy Press, 1999); levee damage from Mary Fran Myers and Gilbert F. White, "The Challenge of the Mississippi Flood," *Environment*, December 1993, pp. 6–9, 25–35.

34. Evolution of Mississippi River management from Hey and Philippi, op. cit. note 33, from Wright, op. cit. note 33, and from Myers and White, op. cit. note 33; artificial channel length from Jeff Hecht, "The Incredible Shrinking Mississippi Delta," *New Scientist*, 14 April 1990, pp. 36–41; flood heights from L.B. Leopold, "Flood Hydrology and the Floodplain," in Gilbert F. White and Mary Fran Myers, eds., *Water Resources Update: Coping with the Flood—The Next Phase* (Carbondale, IL: University Council on Water

Resources, 1994), cited in Richard E. Sparks, "Need for Ecosystem Management of Large Rivers and Their Floodplains," *Bioscience*, March 1995, pp. 168–82; historic flood costs from William Stevens, "The High Costs of Denying Rivers Their Floodplains," *New York Times*, 20 July 1993; 1993 costs from Galloway, op. cit. note 33.

35. U.S. Fish and Wildlife Service (FWS), *Figures on Wetlands Lost in Mississippi Basin Prepared for Post Flood Recovery and the Restoration of Mississippi Basin Floodplains Including Riparian Habitat and Wetlands* (St. Louis, MO: Association of State Wetland Managers, 1993), cited in David S. Wilcove and Michael J. Bean, eds., *The Big Kill: Declining Biodiversity in America's Lakes and Rivers* (Washington, DC: Environmental Defense Fund, 1994); Hey and Philippi, op. cit. note 33; T.E. Dahl, *Wetland Losses in the United States 1780's to 1980's* (Washington, DC: U.S. Department of the Interior (DOI), FWS, 1990); fisheries from Calvin R. Fremling et al., "Mississippi River Fisheries: A Case History," in D.P. Dodge, ed., *Proceedings of the International Large River Symposium, Canadian Special Publication of Fisheries and Aquatic Sciences 106* (Ottawa, ON, Canada: Department of Fisheries and Oceans, 1989), pp. 309–51, and from Joseph H. Wlosinski et al., "Habitat Changes in Upper Mississippi River Floodplain" in E.T. LaRoe et al., eds., *Our Living Resources* (Washington, DC: DOI, National Biological Service, 1995), pp. 234–36; 83 percent from Missouri River Coalition, "Comments on the Missouri River Master Water Control Manual Review and Update Draft Environmental Impact Assessment," 1 March 1995.

36. Hecht, op. cit. note 34; National Marine Fisheries Service, *Fisheries of the United States, 1990* (Washington, DC: U.S. Government Printing Office, 1991), cited in J.M. Hefner et al., *Southeast Wetlands: Status and Trends, Mid-1970s to Mid-1980s* (Atlanta, GA: DOI, FWS, 1994).

37. Deborah Moore, "What Can We Learn From the Experience of the Mississippi?" (San Francisco, CA: Environmental Defense Fund, 7 September 1994); Wright, op. cit. note 33.

38. Missouri River Coalition, op. cit. note 35.

39. Myers and White, op. cit. note 33; flood payments from ASFPM, *National Flood Programs in Review—2000* (Madison, WI: 2000), p. 42, citing National Wildlife Federation analysis "Higher Ground."

40. For summary of task force recommendations, see Myers and White, op. cit. note 33; Galloway, op. cit. note 33; National Research Council (NRC), *Restoration of Aquatic Ecosystems: Science, Technology, and Public Policy* (Washington, DC: National Academy Press, 1992); ASFPM, op. cit. note 39.

41. A.Z.M. Obaidullah Khan, Bangladesh Centre for Advanced Studies, "Bangladesh Floods 1998 and Food Security," paper prepared for the Conference on Natural Disasters and Policy Response in Asia: Implications for Food Security," Harvard University, 30 April–1 May 1999;

Government of Bangladesh, "Damages Caused by Flood 1998 (as of October 4, 1998)," <www.bangladeshonline.com/gob/flood98/_foreign_1.htm>, viewed 1 August 2000, except death and homeless from Red Cross, op. cit. note 14, p. 32; Dixit and Ahmed, op. cit. note 21, pp. 2772–74.

42. Dixit and Ahmed, op. cit. note 21; Khan, op. cit. note 41; climate change impacts from McCarthy et al., op. cit. note 14; "Bangladesh's Sundarbans Forest Threatened by Global Warming: Experts," *Agence France Presse*, 29 August 2000; Alfredo Quarto et al., "Choosing the Road to Sustainability: The Impacts of Shrimp Aquaculture and the Models for Change," prepared for the International Live Aquatics '96 Conference, Seattle, WA, 13–15 October 1996.

43. Hofer cited in Dixit and Ahmed, op. cit. note 21.

44. World coastal population estimates from Joel E. Cohen et al., "Estimates of Coastal Populations," *Science*, 14 November 1997, p. 1209c; U.S. coastal population from Sharon Begley and Thomas Hayden, "Floyd's Watery Wrath," *Newsweek*, 27 September 1999, p. 20; Florida population growth from Dennis S. Mileti, *Disasters by Design: A Reassessment of Natural Hazards in the United States* (Washington, DC: Joseph Henry Press, 1999), p. 42; hurricane frequency from Roger A. Pielke, Jr., "Reframing the US Hurricane Problem," in Roger Pielke, Jr., and Roger Pielke, Sr., eds., *Storms: Vol. 1* (London: Routledge, 2000), p. 391.

45. Molly O. Sheehan, "Urban Population Continues to Rise," in Lester R. Brown, Michael Renner, and Brian Halweil, *Vital Signs 2000* (New York: W.W. Norton & Company, 2000), pp. 104–05; megacities from U.N. Population Division, *World Urbanization Prospects: The 1999 Revision* (New York: 1999).

46. Red Cross, op. cit. note 14, p. 17; Robert Hamilton, "Reducing Impacts of Natural Disasters—Are We Making Any Progress?" presentation for Society for International Development Working Group, Washington, DC, 27 July 2000; Mileti, op. cit. note 44; Kobe from Munich Re, op. cit. note 11, p. 123.

47. G.E. Hollis, "The Effect of Urbanization on Floods of Different Reference Interval," *Water Resources Research*, June 1975, pp. 431–35; G.E. Hollis, "Rain, Roads, Roofs, and Runoff: Hydrology in Cities," *Geography*, vol. 73, no. 1 (1988), pp. 9–18; Munich Re, op. cit. note 10, p. 49.

48. Red Cross, op. cit. note 14, p. 19; Venezuela from Red Cross. op. cit. note 1, p. 99.

49. Venezuela from Red Cross, op. cit. note 1, p. 88; Nicaraguans living below poverty line from Juanita Darling, "For Those Spared by Mitch, Safe Future Hinges on Jobs," *Los Angeles Times*, 3 April 1999; population distribution from World Neighbors, op. cit. note 6.

50. James Wilson and Fiona Ortiz, "Mitch Teaches a Costly Conservation Lesson," *EcoAméricas*, December 1998, pp. 6–8; Red Cross, op. cit. note 14, pp. 42–54; World Neighbors, op. cit. note 6, pp. 8–9.

51. World Neighbors, op. cit. note 6, pp. 8–11.

52. Honduras from Christian Aid, op. cit. note 2; Nicaragua from World Neighbors, op. cit. note 6, p. 7; Organization of American States (OAS), "Hurricane Mitch Affects OAS Land-Mine Removal Efforts," press release (Washington, DC: 9 November 1999).

53. Delayed development and rebuilding costs from U.S. Department of State, op. cit. note 2; debt and service from World Bank, op. cit. note 2.

54. "Bank Unveils New Support for Hurricane Mitch Recovery," *World Bank News*, 17 December 1998; Doug Rekenthaler, "The Battle of Mitch May be Over, But the War Has Just Begun," DisasterRelief.org, <www.disaster relief.org/Disasters/990108Honduras>; Christian Aid, op. cit. note 2; "Debt Relief to Mitch Victims," *BBC Online News*, 11 December 1998.

55. Patricia L. Delaney and Elizabeth Shrader, "Gender and Post-Disaster Reconstruction: The Case of Hurricane Mitch in Honduras and Nicaragua," Decision Review Draft (Washington, DC: World Bank LCSPG/LAC Gender Team, January 2000); Ben Wisner, "Disaster Vulnerability: Scale, Power, and Daily Life," *GeoJournal*, vol. 30, no. 2 (1993), pp. 127–40; migrant workers from Bob Edwards, East Carolina University, presentation at 25th Annual Hazards Research and Applications Workshop, Boulder, CO, 11 July 2000; Mileti, op. cit. note 44, p. 7.

56. Red Cross, op. cit. note 1.

57. Quote from Laurel Reuter, "A Flood of Fire and Ice," *Northwest Report*, December 1997, p. 28; Delaney and Shrader, op. cit. note 55; Elaine Enarson and Betty Hearn Morrow, eds., *The Gendered Terrain of Disaster: Through Women's Eyes* (Westport, CT: Praeger/Greenwood, 1998); Betty Hearn Morrow and Brenda Phillips, eds., *International Journal of Mass Emergencies and Disasters* (Special Issue on Women and Disasters), vol. 17, no 1 (1999); Walter Peacok et al., eds., *Hurricane Andrew: Ethnicity, Gender and the Sociology of Disasters* (London: Routledge, 1997).

58. Delaney and Shrader, op. cit. note 55; Enarson and Hearn Morrow, op. cit. note 57; Hearn Morrow and Phillips, op. cit. note 57.

59. Delaney and Shrader, op. cit. note 55.

60. Wisner, op. cit. note 55; North Carolina from Edwards, op. cit. note 55.

61. Quote from Delaney and Shrader, op. cit. note 55.

62. Disaster assistance budget from Board on Natural Disasters (BOND), "Mitigation Emerges as Major Strategy for Reducing Losses Caused by Natural Disasters," *Science*, 18 June 1999, p. 1947.

63. Mileti, op. cit. note 44, p. 6.

64. World Bank/U.S. Geological Survey (USGS) cited in Twigg, op. cit. note 7; German T. Velasquez et al., "A New Approach to Disaster Mitigation and Planning in Mega-cities: The Pivotal Role of Social Vulnerability in Disaster Risk Management," in Takashi Inoguchi et al., eds., *Cities and the Environment: New Approaches for Eco-Societies* (Tokyo: United Nations University Press, 1999), p. 162.

65. Lessons not learned from L. Comfort et al., "Reframing Disaster Policy: The Global Evolution of Vulnerable Communities," *Environmental Hazards*, vol. 1, no. 1 (1999), pp. 39–44; Nicaraguan government inactivity from "Mitch Worsened by Environmental Neglect," *Environmental News Network*, 19 March 1999; Las Casitas death toll from Red Cross, op. cit. note 14.

66. Red Cross, op. cit. note 1, pp. 88–89.

67. Death toll from Munich Re, op. cit. note 4; inaction from Uday Mahurkar, "Unheeded Death Knell," *India Today*, 22 June 1998.

68. Public health sector response from Meena Gupta, "Cyclone and After: Managing Public Health," *Economic and Political Weekly*, 13 May 2000, pp. 1705–09; deaths and homeless from "Catastrophe!" op. cit. note 4, p. 6; 1 million families from Richard Mahapatra, "A State in Chaos," *Down to Earth*, 15 December 1999, pp. 30–33; Andhra Pradesh versus Orissa from ibid., and from David Gardner, "Orissa Death Toll Doubles as Recriminations Fly," *Financial Times*, 11 November 1999.

69. Gujarat from Martha Ann Overland, "Earthquake Building Codes," *Morning Edition*, National Public Radio, 5 February 2001, and from Roger Bilham, University of Colorado, "26 January 2001 Bhuj Earthquake, Gujarat, India," <cires.colorado.edu/~bilham/Gujarat2001.html>, viewed 16 August 2001; "building amnesties" and "murderers" from Frederick Krimgold, World Institute for Disaster Risk Management, presentation at 25th Annual Hazards Research and Applications Workshop, Boulder, CO, 11 July 2000; Haldun Armagan, "Turkey's Earthquake Exposed a Landscape of Deals and Corruption," *The World Paper*, November 1999, pp. 1–2; USGS, "Implications for Earthquake Risk Reduction in the United States from the Kocaeli, Turkey Earthquake of August 17, 1999," Circular No. 1193 (Denver, CO: 2000).

70. Red Cross, op. cit. note 14; Honduras from Christian Aid, op. cit. note 2; Venezuela from Red Cross, op. cit. note 1, pp. 99–100; Gujarat from Overland, op. cit. note 69, and from Bilham, op. cit. note 69.

71. Italy from Munich Re, op. cit. note 10, p. 31; subsidization from The H. John Heinz III Center for Science, Economics, and the Environment, *The Hidden Costs of Coastal Hazards: Implications for Risk Assessment and Mitigation* (Washington, DC: Island Press, 2000); 25 percent from BOND, op. cit. note 62, p. 1945; damage source from Mileti, op. cit. note 44, pp. 128–32; model codes from ibid., p. 163.

72. Red Cross, op. cit. note 14.

73. Barber and Schweithelm, op. cit. note 4; David Swimbanks, "Forest Fires Cause Pollution Crisis in Asia," *Nature*, 25 September 1997, p. 321; "Jakarta Must Act to Stop Fires Spreading, Watchdog Warns," *Agence France Presse*, 4 August 1999; peat swamp scheme from Sander Thoenes, "In Asia's Big Haze, Man Battles Man-Made Disaster," *Christian Science Monitor*, 28 October 1997.

74. Indonesia from Barber and Schweithelm, op. cit. note 4, p. 3; Orissa from Bishnu N. Mohapatra, "Politics in Post-Cyclone Orissa," *Economic and Political Weekly*, 15 April 2000, pp. 1353–55; Molly Moore, "Mexico's Flood Response Fuels Political Firestorm," *Washington Post*, 12 October 1999.

75. Temperature from McCarthy et al., op. cit. note 14, p. 3; quote from ibid., p. 13; all else from ibid. and from "Technical Summary," in ibid.; Figure 6 based on McCarthy et al., op. cit. note 14, on Revenga et al., op. cit. note 23, and on Robert T. Watson et al., *The Regional Impacts of Climate Change: An Assessment of Vulnerability*, Special Report of IPCC Working Group II (Cambridge, U.K.: Cambridge University Press, 1998).

76. Sea level rise from McCarthy et al., op. cit. note 14, p. 3; The British Meteorological Office, "Predictions of Future Climate Change", <www.met-office.gov.uk/research/hadleycentre/pubs/brochures/b2000/predictions.html>, viewed 21 July 2001; number of people affected from McCarthy et al., op. cit. note 14, p. 13.

77. Sea level rise from McCarthy et al., op. cit. note 14, and from David R. Easterling et al., "Climate Extremes: Observations, Modeling, and Impacts," *Science*, 22 September 2000, pp. 2068–74; Susan Kim, "NYC Flooding Could Be Common in Next Century," *Disaster News Network*, 8 August 1999; Table 1 based on McCarthy et al., op. cit. note 14, pp. 49 (Asia), 611 (Europe), and on Watson et al., op. cit. note 75, pp. 66–67 (Africa), 211 (Latin America), 300 (North America); quote from ibid., p. 6.

78. Figure of $300 billion from Berz, op. cit. note 17; damage to coastal infrastructure from McCarthy et al., op. cit. note 14, p. 13; Asia and quote from ibid., pp. 66, 68.

79. Daniel Sarewitz and Roger Pielke, Jr., "Breaking the Global-Warming Gridlock," *The Atlantic Monthly*, July 2000, pp. 55–64; quote from McCarthy et al., op. cit. note 14, p. 8.

80. BOND, op. cit. note 62, pp. 1943–97; disaster assistance costs from Heinz Center for Science, Economics, and the Environment, op. cit. note 71, p. 13.

81. Mapping from ASFPM, op. cit. note 39; 25 percent from The H. John Heinz III Center for Science, Economics, and the Environment, "Summary," *Evaluation of Erosion Hazards*, April 2000, p. 22.

82. "Forestry Cuts Down on Logging," *China Daily*, 26 May 1998; Zhongwei Guo et al., "Ecosystem Functions, Services, and Their Values—A Case Study in Xingshan County of China," *Ecological Eocnomics*, vol. 38 (2001), pp. 141–54; Hurricane Mitch from World Neighbors, op. cit. note 6.

83. Restoration from NRC, op. cit. note 40, and from Bayley, op. cit. note 21; Mississippi restoration from Hey and Philippi, op. cit. note 33, pp. 4–17; U.K. restoration from Alex Kirby, "Wetlands 'Can Lessen Flood Threat,'" *BBC News Online*, 31 July 2001, and from Royal Society for the Protection of Birds, "RSPB Releases its Vision for a Wildlife-Rich Countryside," 30 July 2001, <www.rspb.org.uk/caffairs/archive/571.htm>, viewed 6 August 2001; U.K. floods from Munich Re, op. cit. note 10, pp. 36–39.

84. Red Cross, "Coastal Environmental Protection: A Case Study of the Vietnam Red Cross," <www.ifrc.org/what/dp/vietnam.asp>, viewed 13 July 2001.

85. *The Cape of Flames*, op. cit. note 30; Working for Water Programme, op. cit. note 30.

86. USGS, op. cit. note 69.

87. India from Krimgold, op. cit. note 69; Bangladesh from Aldo Benini, Global Land Mine Survey, discussion with author, 10 July 2000; Philip R. Berke et al., "Recovery After Disaster: Achieving Sustainable Development, Mitigation, and Equity," *Disasters*, vol. 17, no. 2 (1993), pp. 93–109.

88. North Carolina from Sue Anne Pressley, "In North Carolina, Floyd Leaves a Toxic Legacy," *Washington Post*, 22 September 1999; Mozambique from Trygve Olfarnes, "Mozambique's Plight Moves International Donors," *Choices* (U.N. Development Programme), vol. 9, no. 3 (2000), p. 15; Central America from OAS, op. cit. note 52; Anne Cerimagic, "Floods Bring New Dangers in Bosnia Herzegovina," Red Cross, 27 June 2001, <www.ifrc.org/docs/news/01/062701>.

89. Earl J. Baker, "Hurricane Evacuation in the United States," in Pielke and Pielke, op. cit. note 44, p. 306; Robert L. Southern, "Tropical Cyclone Warning-Response Strategies," in ibid., pp. 286, 297, 298.

90. "Sharing Information Worldwide," session at 25th Annual Hazards Research and Applications Workshop, Boulder, CO, 10 July 2000; Deborah

Shapely, "Weathering Disasters" (Outlook), *Washington Post*, 12 August 2001.

91. Mileti, op. cit. note 44, pp. 11–14.

92. Red Cross, op. cit. note 14; Indonesia from Barber and Schweithelm, op. cit. note 4; Russia from Josh Newell, Anatoly Lebedev, and David Gordon, *Plundering Russia's Far East Taiga: Illegal Logging, Corruption and Trade* (Oakland, CA: Pacific Environment and Resources Center, Bureau for Regional Oriental Campaigns (Vladivostok, Russia), and Friends of the Earth–Japan, 2000).

93. Mileti, op. cit. note 44, p. 8; Munich Re, op. cit. note 11; Berz, op. cit. note 17.

94. National Flood Insurance Program (NFIP) standards from French Wetmore, French and Associates, presentation at 25th Annual Hazards Research and Applications Workshop, Boulder, CO, 11 July 2000; NFIP critique and recommendations from Heinz Center for Science, Economics, and the Environment, op. cit. note 71, and from ASFPM, op. cit. note 39.

95. Red Cross, op. cit. note 14, p. 110; Twigg, op. cit. note 7.

96. Red Cross, op. cit. note 14, pp. 101–14.

97. Red Cross, "Reality Check Needed on International Aid Efforts, Says World Disasters Report 2001," 28 June 2001, <www.ifrc.org/docs/news/01/ 062802/>, viewed 28 June 2001; tied aid and bilateral relief from Red Cross, op. cit. note 1, pp. 43, 168.

98. World Bank, "Reducing 'Preventable' Costs of Natural Disasters Vital for Developing Countries," press release (Washington, DC: 2 February 2000).

99. "Tegucigalpa Declaration Jubilee 2000 Latin America and Caribbean Platform: 'Yes to Life, No to Debt,'" <www.jubilee2000uk.org/latin_ america/declaration.htm>, viewed 31 March 1999; debt from World Bank, op. cit. note 2.

100. Donor pledges from Olfarnes, op. cit. note 88; debt relief from Joseph Kahn, "Wealthy Nations Propose Doubling Poor's Debt Relief," *New York Times*, 17 September 2000, and from "Mozambique Debt Payments Were Suspended by Paris Club of Government Donors," *Humanitarian Times*, 17 March 2000.

101. Christian Aid, op. cit. note 2; "Debt Relief to Mitch Victims," op. cit. note 54; "Paris Club Exposed over 'Misleading' Announcement on Hurricane Mitch Debt Deal," Jubilee 2000 Coalition, <www.jubilee2000uk. org/news/paris2412.html>, viewed 3 March 1999; quote from Oscar Andres

Rodriguez, "Forgive the Debts of Poor Countries" (op ed), *Miami Herald*, 18 March 1999; Joseph Hanlon, "Nicaragua & Honduras Spend as Much on Debt Service as Reconstruction," Jubilee 2000 Coalition, <www.jubilee2000 uk.org/reports/hurricane2910.html>, viewed 17 October 2000.

102. Post-hurricane outlays and International Monetary Fund limits from Hanlon, op. cit. note 101; "Washington Creditors Continue to Squeeze Debt Repayments Out of Victims of Hurricane Mitch," Jubilee 2000 Coalition, <www.jubilee2000uk.org/news/hurricane2910.html>, viewed 17 October 2000.

103. Rodriguez, op. cit. note 101; Jubilee 2000 from <www.jubilee 2000uk.org>; 10 percent from Joe Clancy, "Debt Relief: 'Too Little, Too Slow,'" <CNN.com>, 26 September 2000; 3 percent from Christian Aid, op. cit. note 2. (In contrast, debt service is 32 percent of export revenues in Nicaragua and 21 percent in Honduras; Worldwatch calculations based on World Bank, op. cit. note 2.) Joseph Hanlon, *Debt, Default and Relief in the Past—And How We Are Demanding that the Poor Pay More This Time* (London: Jubilee 2000 Coalition, 1998).

104. Jon Ingleton, ed., *Natural Disaster Management: A Presentation to the International Decade for Natural Disaster Reduction (IDNDR) 1999–2000* (Leicester, U.K.: Tudor Rose, 1999); Gilbert White, "A Decade of Missed Opportunities?" in ibid., pp. 284–85.

105. Roger Pielke, Jr., letter to author, 31 July 2001; United Nations, "Review of the Implementation of Commitments and of Other Provisions of the Convention," FCCC/CP/2001/L.7, prepared for Conference of the Parties, Bonn, 16–27 July 2001.

106. Dixit and Ahmed, op. cit. note 21; Mileti, op. cit. note 44.

The Worldwatch CD-ROM

Put Worldwatch Data to Work on Your Computer with the Worldwatch CD-Rom

The Worldwatch CD-ROM includes statistical data and graphs from all Worldwatch publications over the last three years. With this new product, you can import all the tables, charts and graphs from *Vital Signs*, *State of the World*, Worldwatch Papers, and other Institute publications into your own spreadsheet program, presentation software, or word processor. Just think of the possibilities. You can print out tables and graphs to illustrate lectures or presentations; make your own "what if?" projections; or even create hand-outs for students or conference participants.

Buy the CD-ROM for just $99 and get the award-winning annuals, *Vital Signs 2001* and *State of the World 2001*, FREE (a savings of $29.90).

Features:

• Color-enhanced graphics of data in Microsoft® Excel format from all current Worldwatch publications, including *Vital Signs 2001*, *State of the World 2001*, Worldwatch Papers, and the WORLD WATCH magazine (from June 2000 on).

• Fully searchable text and data of both *Vital Signs 2001* and *State of the World 2001*.

• An archive of all data from Worldwatch publications in Excel format, 1999–2000.

• Easy to read full text versions of *Vital Signs 2001* and *State of the World 2001* in Adobe® pdf format.

• Runs on both PC and Macintosh computers; no special software required.

Use the order form that follows. Order by phone, fax, e-mail, or online:
Phone: (800) 555-2028 or (301) 567-9522 • **Fax:** (301) 567-9553
E-mail: wwpub@worldwatch.org • **Web:** www.worldwatch.org

Worldwatch Papers

No. of Copies

Worldwatch Papers by Janet N. Abramovitz

_____WWP0158 **Unnatural Disasters**
_____WWP0149 **Paper Cuts: Recovering the Paper Landscape** with Ashley Mattoon
_____WWP0140 **Taking a Stand: Cultivating a New Relationship with the World's Forests**
_____WWP0128 **Imperiled Waters, Impoverished Future: The Decline of Freshwater Ecosystems**

Climate Change, Energy, and Materials

_____WWP0157 **Hydrogen Futures: Toward a Sustainable Energy System**
_____WWP0151 **Micropower: The Next Electrical Era**
_____WWP0144 **Mind Over Matter: Recasting the Role of Materials in Our Lives**
_____WWP0138 **Rising Sun, Gathering Winds: Policies to Stabilize the Climate and Strengthen Economies**
_____WWP0130 **Climate of Hope: New Strategies for Stabilizing the World's Atmosphere**

Ecological and Human Health

_____WWP0153 **Why Poison Ourselves? A Precautionary Approach to Synthetic Chemicals**
_____WWP0148 **Nature's Cornucopia: Our Stake in Plant Diversity**
_____WWP0145 **Safeguarding The Health of Oceans**
_____WWP0142 **Rocking the Boat: Conserving Fisheries and Protecting Jobs**
_____WWP0141 **Losing Strands in the Web of Life: Vertebrate Declines and the Conservation of Biological Diversity**
_____WWP0129 **Infecting Ourselves: How Environmental and Social Disruptions Trigger Disease**

Economics, Institutions, and Security

_____WWP0155 **Still Waiting for the Jubilee: Pragmatic Solutions for the Third World Debt Crisis**
_____WWP0152 **Working for the Environment: A Growing Source of Jobs**
_____WWP0146 **Ending Violent Conflict**
_____WWP0139 **Investing in the Future: Harnessing Private Capital Flows for Environmentally Sustainable Development**
_____WWP0137 **Small Arms, Big Impact: The Next Challenge of Disarmament**
_____WWP0134 **Getting the Signals Right: Tax Reform to Protect the Environment and the Economy**
_____WWP0133 **Paying the Piper: Subsidies, Politics, and the Environment**
_____WWP0127 **Eco-Justice: Linking Human Rights and the Environment**
_____WWP0126 **Partnership for the Planet: An Environmental Agenda for the United Nations**
_____WWP0125 **The Hour of Departure: Forces That Create Refugees and Migrants**

Food, Water, Population, and Urbanization

_____WWP0156 **City Limits: Putting the Brakes on Sprawl**
_____WWP0150 **Underfed and Overfed: The Global Epidemic of Malnutrition**
_____WWP0147 **Reinventing Cities for People and the Planet**
_____WWP0143 **Beyond Malthus: Sixteen Dimensions of the Population Problem**
_____WWP0136 **The Agricultural Link: How Environmental Deterioration Could Disrupt Economic Progress**
_____WWP0135 **Recycling Organic Waste: From Urban Pollutant to Farm Resource**
_____WWP0132 **Dividing the Waters: Food Security, Ecosystem Health, and the New Politics of Scarcity**
_____WWP0131 **Shrinking Fields: Cropland Loss in a World of Eight Billion**

_____**Total copies (transfer number to order form on next page)**

PUBLICATION ORDER FORM

NOTE: Many Worldwatch publications can be downloaded as PDF files from our website at **www.worldwatch.org**. Orders for printed publications can also be placed on the web.

_____ *State of the World:* **$15.95**
The annual book used by journalists, activists, scholars, and policymakers worldwide to get a clear picture of the environmental problems we face.

_____ **State of the World Library: $30.00 (international subscribers $45)**
Receive *State of the World* and all Worldwatch Papers as they are released during the calendar year.

_____ *Vital Signs:* **$13.95**
The book of trends that are shaping our future in easy-to-read graph and table format, with a brief commentary on each trend.

_____ **WORLD WATCH magazine subscription: $20.00 (international subscribers $35.00)**
Stay abreast of global environmental trends and issues with our award-winning, eminently readable bimonthly magazine.

_____ **Worldwatch CD-ROM: $99.00**
Contains global agricultural, energy, economic, environmental, social, and military indicators from all current Worldwatch publications. Includes *Vital Signs* and *State of the World* as they are published. CD contains Microsoft Excel spreadsheets 5.0/95 (*.xls) for Windows, and works on both Mac and PC.

_____ **Worldwatch Papers—See list on previous page Single copy: $5.00**
any combination of titles: 2–5: $4.00 ea. • 6–20: $3.00 ea. • 21 or more: $2.00 ea.

$4.00* Shipping and Handling *($8.00 outside North America)*
*minimum charge for S&H; call (800) 555-2028 for bulk order S&H

_____ **TOTAL** (U.S. dollars only)

Make check payable to: Worldwatch Institute, P.O. Box 879, Oxon Hill, MD 20797 USA

❏ Enclosed is my check or purchase order for U.S. $_____

❏ AMEX ❏ VISA ❏ MasterCard _____
                                     Card Number   Expiration Date

signature _____

name _____ **daytime phone #** _____

address _____

city _____ **state** _____ **zip/country** _____

phone: (800) 555-2028   fax: (301) 567-9553   e-mail: wwpub@worldwatch.org
website: www.worldwatch.org

Wish to make a tax-deductible contribution? Contact Worldwatch to find out how your donation can help advance our work.

Worldwatch Papers

No. of Copies

Worldwatch Papers by Janet N. Abramovitz

_____WWP0158 **Unnatural Disasters**
_____WWP0149 **Paper Cuts: Recovering the Paper Landscape** with Ashley Mattoon
_____WWP0140 **Taking a Stand: Cultivating a New Relationship with the World's Forests**
_____WWP0128 **Imperiled Waters, Impoverished Future: The Decline of Freshwater Ecosystems**

Climate Change, Energy, and Materials

_____WWP0157 **Hydrogen Futures: Toward a Sustainable Energy System**
_____WWP0151 **Micropower: The Next Electrical Era**
_____WWP0144 **Mind Over Matter: Recasting the Role of Materials in Our Lives**
_____WWP0138 **Rising Sun, Gathering Winds: Policies to Stabilize the Climate and Strengthen Economies**
_____WWP0130 **Climate of Hope: New Strategies for Stabilizing the World's Atmosphere**

Ecological and Human Health

_____WWP0153 **Why Poison Ourselves? A Precautionary Approach to Synthetic Chemicals**
_____WWP0148 **Nature's Cornucopia: Our Stake in Plant Diversity**
_____WWP0145 **Safeguarding The Health of Oceans**
_____WWP0142 **Rocking the Boat: Conserving Fisheries and Protecting Jobs**
_____WWP0141 **Losing Strands in the Web of Life: Vertebrate Declines and the Conservation of Biological Diversity**
_____WWP0129 **Infecting Ourselves: How Environmental and Social Disruptions Trigger Disease**

Economics, Institutions, and Security

_____WWP0155 **Still Waiting for the Jubilee: Pragmatic Solutions for the Third World Debt Crisis**
_____WWP0152 **Working for the Environment: A Growing Source of Jobs**
_____WWP0146 **Ending Violent Conflict**
_____WWP0139 **Investing in the Future: Harnessing Private Capital Flows for Environmentally Sustainable Development**
_____WWP0137 **Small Arms, Big Impact: The Next Challenge of Disarmament**
_____WWP0134 **Getting the Signals Right: Tax Reform to Protect the Environment and the Economy**
_____WWP0133 **Paying the Piper: Subsidies, Politics, and the Environment**
_____WWP0127 **Eco-Justice: Linking Human Rights and the Environment**
_____WWP0126 **Partnership for the Planet: An Environmental Agenda for the United Nations**
_____WWP0125 **The Hour of Departure: Forces That Create Refugees and Migrants**

Food, Water, Population, and Urbanization

_____WWP0156 **City Limits: Putting the Brakes on Sprawl**
_____WWP0150 **Underfed and Overfed: The Global Epidemic of Malnutrition**
_____WWP0147 **Reinventing Cities for People and the Planet**
_____WWP0143 **Beyond Malthus: Sixteen Dimensions of the Population Problem**
_____WWP0136 **The Agricultural Link: How Environmental Deterioration Could Disrupt Economic Progress**
_____WWP0135 **Recycling Organic Waste: From Urban Pollutant to Farm Resource**
_____WWP0132 **Dividing the Waters: Food Security, Ecosystem Health, and the New Politics of Scarcity**
_____WWP0131 **Shrinking Fields: Cropland Loss in a World of Eight Billion**

_____**Total copies (transfer number to order form on next page)**

PUBLICATION ORDER FORM

NOTE: Many Worldwatch publications can be downloaded as PDF files from our website at **www.worldwatch.org**. Orders for printed publications can also be placed on the web.

_____ *State of the World:* **$15.95**
The annual book used by journalists, activists, scholars, and policymakers worldwide to get a clear picture of the environmental problems we face.

_____ **State of the World Library: $30.00 (international subscribers $45)**
Receive *State of the World* and all Worldwatch Papers as they are released during the calendar year.

_____ *Vital Signs:* **$13.95**
The book of trends that are shaping our future in easy-to-read graph and table format, with a brief commentary on each trend.

_____ **WORLD WATCH magazine subscription: $20.00 (international subscribers $35.00)**
Stay abreast of global environmental trends and issues with our award-winning, eminently readable bimonthly magazine.

_____ **Worldwatch CD-ROM: $99.00**
Contains global agricultural, energy, economic, environmental, social, and military indicators from all current Worldwatch publications. Includes *Vital Signs* and *State of the World* as they are published. CD contains Microsoft Excel spreadsheets 5.0/95 (*.xls) for Windows, and works on both Mac and PC.

_____ **Worldwatch Papers—See list on previous page Single copy: $5.00**
any combination of titles: 2–5: $4.00 ea. • 6–20: $3.00 ea. • 21 or more: $2.00 ea.

$4.00* Shipping and Handling *($8.00 outside North America)*
*minimum charge for S&H; call (800) 555-2028 for bulk order S&H

_____ **TOTAL** (U.S. dollars only)

Make check payable to: Worldwatch Institute, P.O. Box 879, Oxon Hill, MD 20797 USA

❏ Enclosed is my check or purchase order for U.S. $_____

❏ AMEX ❏ VISA ❏ MasterCard _____
                                    Card Number   Expiration Date

signature _____

name _____ **daytime phone #** _____

address _____

city _____ **state** _____ **zip/country** _____

phone: (800) 555-2028   fax: (301) 567-9553   e-mail: wwpub@worldwatch.org
website: www.worldwatch.org

Wish to make a tax-deductible contribution? Contact Worldwatch to find out how your donation can help advance our work.